PRAISE FOR AMERICAN ANIMALS

"True crime heist tales almost inevitably include an idea that is simultaneously brilliant, crazy, and idiotic, and American Animals is no different. What makes this memoir so entertaining and unusual is that one of the college student knuckleheads involved in this fine art robbery also happens to be a gifted writer. Borsuk's coming of age confession is funny, fast-paced, and highly believable."

— Guy Lawson, *New York Times* bestselling author of *War Dogs*

"Eric Borsuk writes beautifully, inhabiting the fertile and scattered minds of these young college students with a style that is both raw and brutally self-aware. The streamlined writing fuels an explosive plot line and the result is a fine book that is spare and literary while also compulsively readable. A literary page turner!"

– Stephen Elliot, bestselling author of *The Adderall Diaries*

"It's an oft-told tale - a group of stoner college friends pull off the daring daytime heist of a rare book library and trigger a transcontinental caper involving the FBI, Christie's auction house and dirtball Dutchmen - but in Eric Borsuk's hands, it's like we're hearing it all for the first time. In all seriousness, Borsuk is a damn fine writer, and he has penned an utterly unique coming-of-age memoir, one that is alternately poignant and hilarious but uniformly brilliant. I can't wait to read the next installment of his life story - one that hopefully doesn't involve another lengthy prison sentence."

"An ill-conceived rare-book heist becomes the chrysalis for a rare sort of book indeed: a true-crime memoir that takes off on the wings of Borsuk's deft prose, dark humor, and often disarming humanity."

"A burningly vibrant, beautifully iconic fast-paced American coming of age heist story."

"American Animals is a book unlike any I've ever read. The twist and turns and audacity can lend themselves to incredulity, but at the heart of this book is a humanness that even those shaking their heads the most will have to recognize. Eric Borsuk's work here is as daring as any heist."

AMERICAN ANIMALS

AMERICAN ANIMALS

A TRUE CRIME MEMOIR

ERIC BORSUK

TURNER PUBLISHING COMPANY

Turner Publishing Company
Nashville, Tennessee
www.turnerpublishing.com

Cover design: Chris Walker
Book design: Tim Holtz

Library of Congress Cataloging-in-Publication Data
Names: Borsuk, Eric, author.
Title: American animals : a memoir / Eric Borsuk.
Description: Nashville : Turner Publishing Company, [2020] | Summary:
    "American Animals is a coming-of-age crime memoir centered around three
    childhood friends: Warren, Spencer, and Eric"– Provided by publisher.
Identifiers: LCCN 2019025030 (print) | LCCN 2019025031 (ebook) | ISBN
    9781684424511 (hardcover) | ISBN 9781684424504 (paperback) | ISBN
    9781684424528 (ebook)
Subjects: LCSH: Transylvania University. Library. | Book
    thefts–Kentucky–Lexington. | College students–Kentucky–Biography. |
    Borsuk, Eric.
Classification: LCC Z733.T76 B67 2020 (print) | LCC Z733.T76
(ebook) |
    DDC 364.16/28002–dc23
LC record available at https://lccn.loc.gov/2019025030
LC ebook record available at https://lccn.loc.gov/2019025031

Printed in the United States of America

17 18 19 20 10 9 8 7 6 5 4 3 2 1

On my view we must suppose that American animals, having in most cases ordinary powers of vision, slowly migrated by successive generations from the outer world into the deeper and deeper recesses of the Kentucky caves.

—Charles Darwin, *On the Origin of Species*

1

ALETHEIA

"Roughly fifty billion species have existed on Earth," the geology professor says, an old gray-haired man with tired eyes, "and almost ninety-nine percent have gone extinct."

Like a stand-up comic bombing on stage, the punchline falls flat.

The lecture hall is painfully silent.

The old man's eyes desperately sweep the audience of aloof freshman faces—yawning, checking their cell phones, thoroughly uninterested in the study of rocks—searching for some sort of reaction to this staggering figure.

"Ninety-nine percent!" he repeats, in case we didn't hear him the first time.

We're in the late Cretaceous—

The Rocky Mountains are taking shape.

A flying reptile with a wingspan of fifty feet soars in the sky.

Much of the planet's petroleum reserves are forming, along with other mineral deposits which will be of commercial value to future civilizations.

Then, somewhere near the end, placental mammals start to evolve. . . .

I scan the classroom for zombies. This is just the kind of place I'd run into them, too. They're usually easy to spot in their fluorescent, popped-collar polos, but I don't recognize anyone. In fact everyone looks about the same. They're all wearing the same self-imposed uniform—same khaki pants, same New Balance running shoes—with the same deadpan expression on their faces. It's like we were packaged and distributed this way, products of a Khaki Generation—bland, off-white, 100% cotton twill.

During the beginning of the semester, I made the mistake of joining a fraternity. Some older guys I knew from high school offered me a bid at the most sought-after frat on campus. I never really saw myself as a frat guy, but I didn't know how to turn it down.

Come on, man! It'll be fun, they said. *Parties, girls what's not to like?*

But it ended up being the crazy, Southern, racist frat—

Suddenly everything in my life was *for the house,* as they say. I became a pledge, a bitch, relegated to long nights in basements being hazed—punched, spit on, pissed on, forced to recite creeds and founding fathers in front of Confederate flags.

When I quit, they put out some sort of mafia-like frat hit on me. Both actives and pledges alike were instructed to fight me anytime they spotted me on campus.

Now, wherever I go, these pastel preps hunt me like zombies.

"It's sixty-six million years ago," the professor excitedly blurts out. "The asteroid is headed straight for us!"

The sky turns red and my blood starts to boil.

———

My cell phone rings to a rendition of Orff's *O Fortuna*, illuminating the otherwise pitch-black bedroom.

It's late, or rather early.

Warren's name is flashing on the screen.

At first, I think I'm still dreaming. We haven't spoken since our argument. It was over money, of all things. Long story short, some cash went missing from my bedroom. When I questioned Warren about the incident, he freaked out, as if I were accusing him of stealing from me. The whole thing was a big misunderstanding. We grew up together—*we were like brothers*. But that was all months ago.

When the voicemail alert chimes, I snatch up the phone—

Warren is drunk and rambling. After all this time, it's strange listening to him speak, like hearing the voice of a dead friend.

He quotes Villon: "In my own country I am in a faroff land. I am strong but have no force or power. I win all yet remain a loser. At break of day I say goodnight. When I lie down I have a great fear of falling."

At the end of the message, Warren says he wants to meet.

―――

The next day, I call Warren's dorm room and his stoner roommate answers—sort of. He doesn't bother to say hello, like most people. Instead he just sits there in silence. At first I think it's the answering machine, until I hear breathing on the other end. Mind you, this isn't the first time it's happened. Trying to have a conversation with him is like pulling teeth. The normal components of social interaction go straight out the window.

After an awkward exchange, I'm able to gather enough information to determine that Warren isn't there. I ask the roommate to let the phone ring when I call back. This way I can leave a message for Warren on the machine.

When I call back, the roommate answers.

I explain again what I'm doing.

Warren is the only person I know who doesn't own a cell phone. I used to get calls all day long from unknown numbers—Warren calling from a pay phone, Warren calling from a bar phone, Warren calling from a stranger's phone—most of which ended abruptly with unfamiliar voices in the background demanding their phones back.

However, if it's *you* who needs to get in touch with *him*, forget it. It's useless trying to track him down. Warren's dorm-room landline is the only way to reach him.

A couple hours later, I get a call from a number I've never seen.

"Hey," Warren says.

"You got my message?" I ask.

"Yeah," he says. "I guess you got mine?"

"Yeah."

The conversation drags on like this for a while— brief, empty utterances—as if we're both waiting for the other one to make the first move, which eventually he does.

"Want to meet?" he asks.

"Meet?"

"Yeah, why not?"

I stutter, trying to think of an excuse, but nothing comes to mind.

"Oh . . . I don't know . . . I just wasn't expecting—"

"Meet me at Pazzo's," he says. "There's something I want to talk to you about."

—

I'm sitting across the table from Warren. He's wearing his signature brown corduroy jacket and devilish grin.

His hair is disheveled, as if he rushed here from some-where. But, then again, I've never known him to look any different.

According to legend, Warren was born about the size of a radish in an acutely premature miracle birth, and the universe has been trying to destroy him ever since. Throughout the years, I've been a bystander when he was struck by cars, and I've lost count of his broken bones and dislocated joints. He's a weasel-like creature, agile, hard to pin down. Somehow, he always manages to escape.

From the start, our attempts at small talk are awk-ward—lots of toe-tapping and feigned smiles. After not speaking to each other for so long, it seems we've lost our timing.

Something about Warren's demeanor seems dif-ferent now, more unhinged. Throughout the night, I repeatedly catch him peeking over his shoulder and scanning the room, as if he's worried someone is watching us.

Hoping to take the edge off, I order a round of beers with my fake ID.

Before our falling out, the two of us were run-ning a lucrative little dorm-room operation selling counterfeit driver's licenses. Using my own software and equipment, I designed and printed the IDs while Warren peddled them to students on campus, of which, there was no shortage. It seemed we had stumbled upon an untapped market and couldn't produce them fast enough.

Before I knew it, Warren started mingling with a shady crowd of criminals who kept trying to pull us in deeper and deeper. That's around the same time my money went missing, and we all know where the story goes from there.

Suddenly it all just disappeared, along with Warren.

After a couple of beers, we both start to loosen up. It's not long before we're recounting old stories. Like that time we started a food fight in the school cafeteria. *Remember that?* I still can't believe Warren actually stood up on the table and yelled "food fight!" It was like a scene straight out of a John Hughes film, especially when the Dean of Students, Warren's nemesis, barged in and literally hauled us off by our necks.

"We need to put this nonsense behind us," Warren says, still laughing about the food-fight story. "Our friendship is too valuable."

I agree.

"There's something I want to tell you," he says. "It's big. It could change our lives forever."

"You can tell me anything."

Warren peeks around the room to make sure that nobody's eavesdropping.

"Spencer and I have been working on something," he says. "But, before I tell you anything else, I need to know if you're in."

I laugh but quickly realize that he's not joking.

"But, I don't even know what I'm signing up for!"

"I just need a *yes* or *no,*" Warren says.

I'm not sure why—maybe friendship, maybe adventure—but I just shrug my shoulders and say, "Yeah, sure, I'm in."

Warren smiles and nods his head, as if he already knew what my answer would be. After a long pause, he looks over his shoulder one last time and takes a deep breath. Then he opens the floodgates—

"I just got back from Amsterdam," he says. "I flew over there on a fake passport that I got from our friend—you know, *the guy.* Spencer and I are going to rob the Rare Book Room at Transy. My dealer in Amsterdam wants Audubon's *Birds of America,* which he thinks I already have. It could be worth ten million dollars. After the heist, we'll take the loot to Europe. We may be on the run. We may never be able to return. We may never see our families again."

———

Late at night, I'm crossing a dark parking lot when I see them coming for me—zombies, the fast kind. They're rushing like rabid dogs, tripping over each other to get to me.

Before I can react, I'm down on the pavement, all scraped up, fist-fighting an old pledge brother I barely even know. He reeks of bourbon and Polo cologne. I remember hearing once that he was an all-state wrestling champion in high school, and it shows.

At some point in the fight my head bashes against the concrete, and suddenly I am somewhere else. Strange, distant memories flash in my mind, long forgotten, but preserved for some obscure purpose—

The ancient Greek word ἀλήθετα.

A portrait of Philippus Aureolus Theophrastus Bombastus von Hohenheim. *Alle dinge sind gift,* he says. All things are poison.

Ten to the fortieth power.

I can be anywhere, I tell myself.

I am bleeding.

2
ALL THAT IS GOLD

Late-morning sunlight and the warbling of songbirds creeps inside my tent, somewhere deep in the mountains of northern Georgia. Cocooned in a sleeping bag, I plead with myself to get up off the ground, but my body is stiff and sore from long days of backpacking on the Appalachian Trail. Not to mention, I'm still recovering from my latest frat-boy beatdown.

Rubbing gunk from my eyes, I unzip the tent and slip on my boots, carefully maneuvering around a raw-skinned heel blister.

On the opposite side of the fire pit, Warren is dangling between two trees in a hammock, still asleep. Spencer, however, is nowhere to be found.

At first, I just presume he's birdwatching. It's not unusual for him to slip off early in the morning with his binoculars and sketch pad in hand. Sometimes you'll be in the middle of a conversation with him only to find that you've been talking to yourself the entire time. When you turn around, he's gone, tracking down a seductive trill. *You hear that?* he asks, even though you never do. He points, but you can never seem to find it. *Sounds like a . . .* and he inevitably inserts some ridiculous-sounding name, like a tufted titmouse or a white-breasted nuthatch, while hurriedly sketching the bird and adding it to his register of sightings.

The only thing I can't figure out is why Spencer would bring all of his backpacking gear to go birdwatching.

Nearby, I scale a large boulder overlooking the mountainside, tiptoeing around a group of rattlesnakes sunning themselves on the rocks. The Appalachians span the horizon, draped in a plush, green Chattahoochee carpet, while a sweet scent clings to the breeze. It's a beautiful sight, but there's still no sign of Spencer.

Back at camp, I wake Warren and give him the news. After talking it over, we both agree that Spencer never would have brought his fully loaded, sixty-plus pound backpack with him to go birdwatching. That said, we can't figure out why he would've left without telling us, either. That's Backpacking 101: don't abandon your best friends in the middle of the woods. Not to mention, he took our only map and water pump.

With Spencer gone, everything feels off-balance. The three of us have been close friends since our early teens when we each made the cut on a local soccer team. From the start, we all just clicked. Something about our three-sided friendship felt durable, like the sides of a triangle, the most stable shape.

On the count of three.

Warren and I start packing and cooking breakfast, agreeing that if Spencer hasn't returned by the time we're finished, then we'll have no choice but to leave without him.

Delaying the inevitable, I prepare for the day's hike while dragging out every little detail.

One.

I apply sunscreen.

Two.

I apply bug spray.

Two and a quarter.

I attend to my blisters.

Two and a half.

I stretch.

Two and three-quarters.

I stretch some more, all the while looking around for Spencer.

Three.

Having stalled for as long as possible, Warren and I reluctantly hit the trail, leaving a note for Spencer under a rock, in case he returns to the campsite. It's a long shot, but we don't have much of a choice.

All day long, the trail steeply climbs and descends, with no sign of flat earth in sight. Before long it's back to the same old grind, traipsing through rough terrain in ungodly Southern heat, frequently questioning my decision to embark on such a journey in the first place.

Dehydrated and exhausted, we go without speaking for long stretches of time. It's just me, my thoughts, and vast thickets of rhododendron. Naturally, my mind wanders back home to Lexington—

Back to cul-de-sacs of McMansions in gated communities.

Back to strip malls and chain restaurants.

Back to soft white men sipping on small-batch bourbon while "playing the ponies."

Back to a life scripted like a character in a play.

Just do what you're told, they say—

Pray this way.

Walk this way.

Talk this way.

Learn this way.

Think this way.

Work this way.

Shop this way.

Eat this way.

Dress this way.

Vote this way.

Fuck this way.

Love this way.

Hate this way.

Die this way.

After my initial meeting with Warren, I realized that he and Spencer actually had no working plan for the robbery. Apparently it all started when Spencer, along with other incoming art students, was given a tour of the Rare Book Room, a special collections museum inside the library of Transylvania University, also known as Transy, the private liberal-arts college he attends. It's just a few miles down the road from the University of Kentucky, where Warren and I go to school. During the tour, the curator, a friendly, grandma-like librarian named Betty, mentioned that an identical set had recently sold at auction for nearly twelve million dollars. Then one day, Spencer made an offhand remark about the millions of dollars' worth of artwork just sitting inside the museum, and a lightbulb went off in Warren's head.

After a cursory inspection of the premises, Warren deemed the robbery doable and started asking around about how to sell stolen artwork. One of his shady acquaintances hooked him up with an underworld go-between in Manhattan, known only as "The Man in the Green Scarf." Like a scene straight out of a crime film, they met on a bench in Central Park, just outside of The Plaza Hotel, while Spencer kept watch from a distance with his birding binoculars. For a modest fee, the dapper dealer connected them with his associates in the Netherlands.

Shortly after, Warren flew to Amsterdam and met with a black-market art dealer at a coffee shop near Dam Square, claiming to be the representative of a man named Walter Beckman, a private collector out of Boston, who intended to unload some of his personal stash. Though dismayed by Warren's youth—and the fact that he hadn't brought any manuscripts, pictures, or documentation—the dealer maintained that if the so-called Mr. Beckman could produce said artifacts, they would be in business.

The only problem was that Warren and Spencer didn't know how to steal the books. That's what they needed me for. They hoped that my meticulous nature, along with an extensive knowledge of heist-film minutiae, would help them formulate a plan. That's ultimately why the three of us decided to spend our summer break backpacking the Appalachian Trail. It was supposed to be a team-building exercise. That is, until Spencer disappeared.

Late in the afternoon, Warren and I come to a road crossing. It's the first sign of civilization in days. Drenched in sweat, we sit down on the guide rails, while sipping on our last drops of water.

On the opposite side of the road, the trail recedes into the woods up a steep and steady incline. At this rate, we won't make it to the next shelter until after nightfall.

Without thinking, I turn to Warren and say, "Want to hitchhike?"

What started as a joke, purely out of exhaustion, soon turns into an actual plan. It's completely unrealistic, but we decide to thumb it to the nearest town in search of supplies. From there, we'll work our way back to the trail, hopefully ahead of Spencer (assuming he's still heading north), and travel south until we find him. That's the plan, at least.

The first driver, a woman in a Subaru, actually accelerates when she sees us standing on the side of the road, grinning with our thumbs in the air. Assuming it's an isolated incident, we continue to try our luck. But after a few more unsuccessful attempts, I figure out the problem—it's me.

I watch as a man in a truck slows down for Warren, but then, upon spotting me, instantly speeds off.

Intrigued, I look Warren up and down. He's your all-American boy next-door—athletic, clean-shaven, spotless, and even wearing brand-new hiking clothes.

Then, using an emergency signal-mirror, I proceed to examine my own reflection—I'm bearded, about twenty pounds overweight, wearing dark sunglasses, a boonie hat, and covered head-to-toe in dirt. I am the complete opposite of Warren, and not someone you would want to pick up on the side of a remote mountain road—or any road for that matter! It's a troubling discovery that leaves me with only one option: I'll have to hide in the woods, out of sight.

Peeking through tree branches, I watch Warren sluggishly kicking rocks up and down the highway. It's been about an hour since our last failed attempt. I'm pouring sweat and losing hope. *We might just have to accept the inevitable,* I think to myself, when suddenly I hear the faint hum of an engine coming around the bend.

Wading through brush, I catch a glimpse of Warren huddled over the window of an old hatchback. Before I know it, he's waving me over.

Frantically, I gather my gear and stumble out of the forest, lumbering toward the car like some mythical woodland beast. Warren is already settled in up front, so I cram into the backseat.

"Thanks for stopping," I say, while trying not to make eye contact.

The driver, a long-haired Hispanic man in a tank top, stares back at me with a puzzled expression on his face, like he can't figure out what is happening. Clearly having second thoughts, the man sits there for a moment, deliberating with himself. Then, surprisingly, he turns back around and shifts the car into drive.

Once we're coasting down the windy, mountain road, Warren tells him that we have no idea where we are. "Just trying to get to the nearest town," he says. "Wherever that is."

But the man says nothing, just glances back at me in the rearview mirror, with a little teardrop tattoo visible underneath his right eye.

I'm racking my brain trying to remember what it means. Did he?

     a) Kill someone?

     b) Lose someone?

     c) Do time?

     d) All of the above

We drive for a while in silence, eventually turning onto a rugged, one-lane backroad—then another, and another. Soon, we're deep in the woods, traversing creeks on rickety old bridges, and passing decrepit log cabins barely withstanding the incursion of time.

"Some sort of shortcut?" I ask.

Still, the man says nothing. Yet as I shift nervously in my seat, the teardrop-tattooed eye watches my every move.

In the passenger-side mirror, I see Warren shooting me a crazed look and nodding his head down to the side, calling attention to an unsheathed hunting knife in his right hand.

Suddenly, time slows to a crawl—

I brace myself for something terrible to happen, a scene of bloody chaos. As usual, I do nothing—I don't intervene. I just follow Warren's lead and remind myself to grab the steering wheel when shit goes down so we don't drive off the cliff.

Then, out of nowhere, the shady forest opens up to a bright, sunny sky, and all of a sudden we're driving down the main strip of a small mountain town.

I panic and open the door while the car is still moving—the outside world loudly rushes in.

As a result, the man swerves the car to the side of the road, shouting at me in Spanish.

Flustered, Warren and I hurriedly drag our packs to the curb, waving and thanking the man for the ride.

But I don't think he hears us over the screeching tires as he speeds away.

As we set off down the sidewalk, our hope of finding supplies quickly fades. The town is small, consisting of only a few basic shops. With no choice but to keep moving, we top off our water bottles in a gas-station restroom and stagger aimlessly along the highway toward the mountains, engulfed in sweltering Southern heat.

At a roadside stand, Warren and I devour an entire bag of peaches like wild animals. When the two of us catch glimpses of each other—our faces plastered in pulp—we completely lose control. Undoubtedly, the outburst had been building up for days, the culmination of endless hours of torment and silence. As we laugh uncontrollably in the bright summer sunlight, holding onto each other for balance, the old man who sold us the fruit slowly backs away, keeping his distance in case whatever we have is contagious.

Across the highway, deep in the forest, I spot lights—shiny, dancing diamonds—flickering between the pine trees. At first, I assume it's just the heat getting to me. It takes a moment before I realize that I'm staring at a lake.

Under the confused gaze of the peach vendor, Warren and I scamper off into the forest, frantically pushing through dense undergrowth in search of water.

We drop our packs on the shore, strip down to nothing, and plunge heedlessly into the lake, as if the murky water could magically solve all of our problems—and somehow it kind of does.

After setting up camp at the water's edge, we devote the remainder of the afternoon to swimming and smoking joints. All throughout the day, gawking families in RVs drive by, berating us in southern accents for taking up prime lakeside real estate with our tents. Nearby, they attach their rattling beasts to electrical outlets. It's not long before the simulcasted clamor of NASCAR overtakes the campsite.

At dusk, we follow the crowds up a grassy hillside to find a field of brightly-lit carnival rides enveloped in the stench of deep-fried meat and sulfur from fireworks exploding overhead.

Wild-eyed carnies casually operate convulsing machines to haunting tunes. They nod at us when we walk past, as if we're kin.

"Lookin' for work?" one of them asks, with a cigarette dangling from his mouth. He says he'll show us the ropes, though what the ropes consist of is unclear. We could travel with him, he says, from town to town, living as carnival folk.

I envision my carnie-self years from now, shirtless, in a denim vest, with the obligatory cigarette wedged between my lips. Seated at the cockpit of The Gravitron, I'm grinning and turning dials like some twisted maestro in the eye of a violent storm. Hordes of hillbillies whirl around me, writhing up and down the walls to extreme centrifugal force, while the southern rock hit "Devil Went Down to Georgia" blares from my cassette boom box.

It's the kind of opportunity that doesn't come along every day, but after careful consideration, we're forced to decline the offer, explaining that our friend is missing and we have to keep searching for him.

———

The next morning, we try our hands—or rather, our thumbs—at hitchhiking once again. By late in the afternoon, not a single car has stopped, and a long stretch of shimmering highway recedes from view. Struggling to stay upright, Warren and I scour the woods for tree branches, using our pocketknives to whittle walking sticks. We have fully accepted our fate of camping alongside the road for the night, when suddenly a big, black tour bus comes barreling past us. At the last second, I stick out my thumb, and amazingly the bus pulls over to the side of the road.

At first, the two of us just stand there, stunned, staring at each other with our mouths open. Then, instinctively, we both start running toward the bus, in case they caught a glimpse of me and start having second thoughts.

Warren makes it to the door just before me. From inside the bus, I hear his muffled voice blurt out, "Holy shit!" When I reach the top of the stairs, I find a scene of hysteria unfolding. What starts as a faint reverberation quickly turns into an entire bus-full of children pointing and shouting—*Awwwwwwww!*—in response to Warren's remark, much like the inevitable uproar that occurs when a classmate is sent to the principal's office.

The chaperone—a balding, overly animated thirty-something—uses hand gestures to quiet the kids like an orchestra conductor, narrowly avoiding all-out anarchy.

"It's your lucky day," he says, winking at us. "We don't normally pick up hitchhikers, but every Tuesday we try to do something nice for someone in need. So, it's Tuesday . . . and you fellows sure look like you're in need."

The man, a local youth minister, is treating his church-camp group to a picnic at a nearby state park. He can't help with our supply needs but offers to drop us off at a spot near the Appalachian Trail. Seeing how we've already wandered this far, it seems like our best option.

As we drag our backpacks down the aisle, the children wait breathlessly to see where we sit. There are only a few open seats, so Warren and I split up.

Toward the back of the bus, I plop down next to a little boy with glasses. Out the corner of my eye, I can see him staring at me, open-mouthed, as if an alien just sat down next to him.

The Lord of the Rings is playing on an overhead monitor. Gandalf the Grey is delivering one of his many eloquent monologues. The little boy says he's memorized all the books and movies word-for-word, which he proves in excruciating detail.

Then, all of a sudden, in a raspy little southern accent, he turns to me and asks, "Are you a wanderer?"

Exhausted, I slump down in the seat and close my eyes. The air conditioning is blasting, ice-cold. Before I know it, I'm drifting in and out of sleep with my head bobbling around uncontrollably. Every now and then I wake to find the boy reciting passages that in my dreamy state sound more like Eastern philosophy than fantasy film.

After sleeping for what feels like hours, I'm jolted awake by the bus pulling to a halt on the side of the road.

"This is as far as I can take you boys," the youth minister shouts back to us.

Disoriented, I fumble together my gear while saying goodbye to the children. Meanwhile, it's clear that something has come over the boy. He looks flustered, like he wants to tell me something but doesn't know how. As I turn to leave, the little bug-eyed Buddha grabs my arm, looks me straight in the eye, and in quite possibly the most transcendent moment of my entire life, quotes Tolkien:

"All that is gold does not glitter," he says, like an oracle Opie Taylor. "Not all those who wander are lost."

There's no telling how long we stare at each other—it could have been a couple of seconds or a lifetime.

———

After sunset, a violent squall surges over the ridgeline, barraging us with hail and fierce wind. We frantically gather our gear in the dark and scramble down the mountainside for cover. With lightning and trees crashing down all around us, Warren and I eventually reach lower ground in the midst of a steady downpour.

Tired and wringing-wet, we slog along for hours in search of the nearest shelter. At every murky bend, I think to myself, *It's got to be just around the corner,* only to find more dark, muddy trail. It's a daunting cycle with no end in sight, until finally, late in the night, I see moonlight reflecting off an old tin roof.

Turning down a side trail, I hear what sounds like children laughing—faint yelps obscured by the constant drumming of rainfall—but quickly dismiss the thought. The woods are full of inexplicable noises. *Just my imagination,* I assume, until I see inside the cabin.

The place has been overrun by a couple dozen prepubescent Boy Scouts, most of whom are running around the cramped shelter playing tag. Some of them are perched up in the rafters, carving their names into the wooden beams with pocketknives. Meanwhile, a shady splinter group in the corner is dumping bags of shredded mozzarella cheese onto the dirt floor and shoving handfuls into their Kool-Aid-stained mouths. When they spot us standing in the doorway—drenched and trying to make sense of the chaotic, lantern-lit scene—the cabin falls silent.

An old man, dressed in a brown forest-ranger uniform, is seated cross-legged on the floor, twisting the gray, wiry ends of his handlebar mustache. He's engaged in a lively conversation with himself, going back and forth, weighing all the viewpoints like an impartial mediator, when the sudden silence breaks his concentration.

"Good day, fellow woodsmen!" he shouts, staggering to his feet and rushing toward us.

Suddenly we're face-to-face with the old man, so close that I can smell his breath, which reeks of mozzarella cheese; there are little globs of the stuff plastered within the crevices of his yellow teeth. I have no idea why he's standing so close to us, or why he's whispering now.

"This whole thing started as a favor for a friend," he says, peeking over his shoulder at the watchful children, as if he were their prisoner. "But I seem to have bitten off more than I can chew."

After a while, the little hellions return to their games, some switching stations, others creating new ones on the spot.

Watching anarchy unfold in the background, I come to a devastating realization: We can't stay here. The place is packed to the brim, with no extra space whatsoever. This means we'll have to hike through the night, in the dark and pouring rain, to the next shelter, nearly eight miles away.

When I whisper this to Warren (don't ask me why I'm whispering now as well), a fearful expression spreads over the old man's face. It's a look that clearly says: *Don't leave me here with them!* So, he attempts to lure us in with bait.

"You boys fancy a smoke? I've got a pipe and some tobacco! How does that sound?"

But it's already late, and we have a long night ahead of us.

Before we leave, the old man asks us for advice, but neither one of us can think of anything to say.

Back on the trail, things start to go downhill quickly, figuratively speaking. My blisters have reached the point of no return—red, raw skin, grating against my boots. Every step feels like searing needles stabbing into my heels. To make matters worse, I feel a muscle cramp coming on, something I'm familiar with from years of playing soccer. I was known as the teammate who always got cramps. It would usually start in my calves, first one, then the other, both muscles clenched in endless contraction, inevitably spreading to my hamstrings, then quads, and eventually my entire body. Without fail, I'd be on a breakaway, just me and the keeper, an easy goal. Then, suddenly, it would be like a sniper had picked me off—my body falling lifelessly to the ground. "Shooter in the clock-tower!" Warren would yell from across the field, laughing uncontrollably.

I writhe around on the trail, convulsing in unnatural movements. Using a rhododendron for support, I try to pull myself up from the ground, only to come crashing back down into the mud when my whole body seizes up. I flick on my headlamp and call for Warren, but he's too far ahead to hear me.

I'll just have to wait it out, I decide, while gnashing my teeth in pain.

Exhausted, I close my eyes and sink into the mud. Every time I think it can't possibly rain any harder, it does, causing large puddles to form around my body. It's uncomfortable at first, but once I stop resisting, it's really not so bad—soothing even, like dissolving into the earth. Eventually, I doze off. . . .

When I wake up, a thick fog has crept in, restricting my view to only a few feet, while enclosing me in a cramped bubble of misty headlamp glare and billions of beating raindrops.

Moments ago, I could've sworn I'd heard grunting sounds in the distance, though it's possible I dreamed it. I've nearly dismissed the thought when suddenly I hear the noise again, this time louder and closer—abrupt snorts and squeals flanking me in the darkness.

Lifting myself up off the ground, I stumble down the slippery trail, trying to keep my legs straight to stave off cramps. Meanwhile, the puzzle pieces are starting to come together. A little ways back I came across a patch of upturned earth. I didn't think much about it at the time, but now it makes perfect sense: Wild boars are known to dig up soil in search of roots and bulbs. Any moment now, one of the vicious, sharp-tusked beasts could burst through the fog and take me out at the knees.

I turn off my headlamp and pick up the pace, adrenaline pushes me through the pain. I'm practically running down the trail. Maybe running isn't the right word, rather, moving as fast as possible through complete darkness with blisters, muscle cramps, and sixty pounds of gear strapped to my back.

Carried along by some innate survival instinct, I lose track of time, and the night turns into one long and foggy daze. In my mind, the boars have all merged into one unified beast—a great amorphous, even-toed ungulate surrounding me in the dark.

Just stay ahead of it, I tell myself, even when the squeals are far behind me. *Just keep moving and don't look back.*

It's late in the night when I finally reach the shelter. By now the adrenaline has worn off, and every part of me feels cold and waterlogged. All I can think about is collapsing.

On the far side of the lean-to, a campfire flickers against the black forest. Two bodies are sprawled out next to the flames, stained red like bleary figures in an oil painting, unspeaking and still.

When I cross the threshold, one of the figures shoots upright. I recognize his voice before anything else.

"Look who I found!" Warren says, pointing to the body lying next to him.

The young man's face glows red against the fire, gaunt and angular. I stare at him blankly, but nothing registers. He grins and waits for me to say something. It takes a moment before he finally comes into focus.

Every aspect of Spencer's appearance is tweaked, as if he's been swapped for a scrawny look-alike. I've never seen him so thin. Even his voice sounds different, deeper, and more strung-out. Apparently he's been pushing over twenty miles a day, which is how he lost so much weight. He says that Warren and I were holding him back. We tend to move at a more leisurely pace, taking in the scenery, while Spencer is more focused on meeting the daily quota of trekked miles. As the days passed, Warren and I kept waking up later and later, until finally one morning Spencer was gone. He claims to have warned us that he would take off if we didn't pick up our pace, but neither of us recalls such a threat.

3
PREREQUISITES

I wake up early one morning to register for classes online, but there's no internet connection.

I restart my computer—*nothing*.

I reboot the router—*still nothing*.

Finally, I troubleshoot—*You are not connected to the internet. The page can't be displayed.*

I try everything, but nothing works.

I scream.

I panic.

I throw on some clothes and sprint through campus to the university library, but by the time I find an open computer and log into my student account, nearly all the classes have filled up. To keep my student loans, I have to stay above a certain number of course hours per semester. As a result, I'm forced to sign up for classes like Tennis and Jiu Jitsu, just to stay enrolled, even though the credits won't apply toward my major—which, by the way, is Accounting, a subject I couldn't possibly care less about.

Ever since I was young, when my uncle started working for the FBI, I had been completely obsessed with the idea of one day becoming an agent myself. This was around the same time that *The X-Files* first aired on television, and instantly I knew it was the career for me. I read every book about the Bureau that I could get my hands on, and I even wrote letters to ex-agent authors asking for advice on how to follow in their footsteps. My plan was to apply to the FBI immediately after graduation. Seeing how the only bachelor's degrees accepted straight out of college were Law and Accounting, it made for an easy choice of a major.

Then, at some point, all of that changed.

As if the transformation occurred seamlessly overnight, I suddenly found myself on the opposite side of the law, immersed in a life of crime for no apparent reason. One day I came across an article about a study that analyzed the brain scans of criminals in comparison to law enforcement officers—the two were nearly identical. *Maybe that has something to do with it,* I wondered.

Before I knew it, I was majoring in something I didn't care about, dedicating my life to something I didn't believe in, forced into years of pointless prerequisites, and, as a result, shackled to a disproportionate debt that I'll never be able to pay back. All that would still be fine and dandy, except I can't even enroll in the pointless prerequisites because I've suddenly lost internet connection at the very moment that thousands of other students are signing up for the exact same classes.

That's how you find yourself standing on a tennis court, lined up side-by-side with a couple dozen other hopeless undergrads. You're practicing your serve—actually, not even the serve, just the toss.

Tennis balls are flying everywhere, some too high, some too low, some not even close—

Concentrate! Don't take your eye off the ball . . . watch it rising high in the gray Kentucky sky . . . lose yourself in the fuzzy, yellow felt . . . nothing else matters except this fleeting moment . . . just make sure that you follow through with your tossing hand.

The ball bounces a couple of times, then rolls away.

Up, down, up, down, up, down.

Chase and repeat.

Your footing changes, and you find yourself standing on a padded blue mat, wearing a heavy cotton jacket called a *gi*. It costs one hundred dollars, and you can't take the class without it. You didn't know that before you signed up for the class—but, then again, you never really had much of a choice, did you?

You're still trying to figure out how to tie the belt when the instructor shouts at you.

"Next up," he says. "Forward roll."

You dart to the line and execute a quick Daniel Larusso-like tuck-and-roll, springing to your feet in fighting stance.

"Well done," the instructor says, seemingly surprised.

Before long, you're lying in the fetal position, practicing something called "shrimping," an evasive technique to avoid being mounted.

"Shrimp!" the instructor yells, as the entire class wiggles around the mat like freshly caught crustaceans on the deck of a fishing trawler.

After the group demonstration, you're paired up with a preppy-looking white boy—

You've mounted him. You're choking him.

He's supposed to be using his newly acquired shrimping skills to escape your grip, but he's not strong enough.

You imagine he's a zombie and start squeezing harder.

He squirms around, eyes bulging.

"You can do it," you encourage him. "Just remember to control your breathing."

———

Early in the morning, an erratic, crinkling sound trickles through the quiet house, lingering in the background at first, then louder and louder, until it's the only thing I can hear.

Please stop. Please stop. Please stop.

I hate it. I want to destroy it, whatever it is.

I'm staring up at the white, popcorn ceiling, losing my mind. Just when I think it's over, and I fall back asleep, the mysterious racket starts back up again.

Groggy and hungover, I force myself out of bed, tiptoeing around bloated male carcasses, occasionally stepping in sticky puddles of spilled hooch.

A porno is playing on the television. It's one of those huge, boxy big-screen TVs, which somehow found its way from the early '90s into our living room. "Oh, God! Right there! That's the spot!" the bushy, blonde-haired actress moans on the screen. Judging by the image quality and excess pubic hair, someone must've discovered our communal vintage-VHS collection.

The house looks like a natural disaster site. There's wreckage scattered everywhere—pizza boxes, cell phones, beer bottles, disposable plastic cups, wallets, random articles of clothing, and several motionless bodies. Not to mention someone left the front door wide open, revealing a blast radius extending all the way out to the street.

In the front yard, a disoriented young man is combing through the debris like a shell-shocked survivor searching for remnants of his belongings. Eventually he gives up and staggers off to some cockroach-infested corner of campus to undoubtedly do it all over again tonight.

Lately it's like our place has become a boarding-house for student delinquents. The doors are never locked, and strangers come and go freely at all hours of the day. For the right price, rooms are available to rent on a month-by-month basis, and each deal is negotiated separately.

Chas, a classmate from high school, oversees the house. He's a snobby rich kid, raised on day-trading and get-rich-quick schemes. His hustler father finances properties and occasionally allows him to manage them. Chas's bedroom, which occupies the entire second floor of the house, is decorated with gangster film posters like *Goodfellas* and *Scarface*. A knock-off katana sword rests on a wall rack, while pistols, shotguns, and throwing stars are stashed in various nooks. Titles like *The Art of War* and *The 48 Laws of Power* line the bookshelf. However, most of the space is occupied by a top-of-the-line home theater system, a California king mattress draped in mulberry silk, and a hefty freshwater aquarium that seems to be stocked only with predatory fish. At odd hours of the day, the old house rattles to the commotion of chaotic action-movie scenes blaring from up above. Every now and then Chas emerges from his loft, dressed in a robe and slippers, like some landlord mobster squeezing us for rent money.

One of the other tenants, an obese country boy from Georgia known only as "Cooter," recently came home with a puppy. After spotting an ad in the classifieds about a newborn litter, he hauled his rusty old Jeep out to a nearby farm to investigate. The breeder couldn't possibly have known any details about Cooter's life, or surely he never would have sold him a living creature. From what I've heard, he hasn't been to class in weeks, and his GPA is hovering just a few tenths of decimals above zero. He's a hulking, sweaty beast of a Southern brute, whose migrations are trailed by various nauseating odors. His appearance alone should have prevented the transaction, but clearly that was not the case. To make matters worse, one day Cooter called everyone into the living room for a house meeting to announce that he had named the poor little brindle boxer "Dixie."

Having tracked down the noise to the laundry room, I stand in the doorway, watching a giant bag of puppy food shake erratically on the floor.

"What's going on here?" I say in a booming voice.

Suddenly the bag stops moving.

After a long pause, Dixie slowly creeps out, cowering and wiggling her little nub of a tail.

I stand over her, scowling, with my arms folded.

"Un-uh, I don't think so, little missy! What do you think this is, an all-you-can-eat buffet?"

Overwrought, her backside starts gyrating uncontrollably, propelling her in circles around the room. Seeing that I'm not buying it, she hams up the performance, making a whole production of it, convulsing and emitting a high-pitched moaning sound before collapsing into the communal laundry pile.

Heaving the heavy dog-food bag on top of the washing machine, I tell her that she's being unreasonable.

Even in her underdeveloped puppy mind, she should know that this eating arrangement is absurd.

Recently, it came to my attention that Cooter is pledging the zombie fraternity. To my knowledge, they haven't figured out that I'm one of his roommates—*not yet, at least*. The point is, Cooter spends all of his time at the frat house now, which means he's never around to take care of Dixie. Lately, he's just been leaving the bag of puppy food open on the floor so that she can feed herself.

Needless to say, I've been gradually taking over responsibilities—

I feed her.

I walk her.

I clean up all her messes.

I let her sleep in my bed (which, incidentally, often involves cleaning up her messes as well, requiring, on more than one occasion, a trip to the dry cleaner).

Not to mention, the biggest job of them all: knowing where she is at all times.

This may seem like a trivial task, but I assure you it's not. With people constantly coming and going in and out of the house, oftentimes leaving doors wide open, watching Dixie is a full-time job. She's an escape artist and hands down the most athletic creature I've ever seen. All day long she bides her time, watching vigilantly as doors swing open and closed. Then, when you least expect it, she bolts—

The alert goes out immediately—*All hands on deck! We're at DIXIECON 1! This is the real thing, folks! This is not a drill.*

Everyone drops what they're doing and rushes outside. It takes multiple people to catch her. By yourself, you don't even stand a chance.

Right away Dixie hops a couple of fences and disappears into the dense, suburban jungle of adjacent backyards. Honestly, in my opinion, your best bet is to follow the screams. With so much pent-up energy releasing all at once, it's not uncommon for Dixie to be mistaken for a rabid marsupial, which means that time is of the essence.

Sometimes I'm lying in bed and barely even clothed, when suddenly I find myself running down the street in the middle of the night, as if I woke up this way, transported from somewhere ill-defined, chasing an elusive creature that only wants to be free.

———

I'm helping Warren carry boxes downstairs to the basement. It's a dark and dingy pit burdened by an ominous presence and an unsecured cellar door that allows rodents to come and go as they please. The one night Spencer slept down there, he suffered his old childhood nightmare. When I pressed him for details, he clammed up, muttering something about evil spirits and how it had been over a decade since he'd last had the dream.

Apparently, Warren finagled a deal with Chas to rent the room for cheap, an arrangement that works out well for both of them. This way, Warren gets a bedroom to himself while paying next to nothing (the bargain-basement deal, if you will), and Chas collects revenue on an otherwise unrentable space.

After descending the staircase, the first area you enter is the "living room," the centerpiece of Warren's lair, decorated with an assortment of mismatched bohemian furniture, coffee tables, lamps, and rugs—all of which he stole from various thrift stores around town.

Throughout the basement, bedsheets hang from the rafters, crudely dividing the open floor plan into a maze of ill-defined rooms carpeted with artificial turf, while the concrete walls are lined with stacked bookshelves and several pieces of original artwork on loan from Spencer as housewarming gifts.

In the corner, next to the sump pit, Warren's bedroom consists of nothing more than a cheap mattress on the floor surrounded by piles of dirty laundry and comic books.

Nearby, he's converted an old workbench into a study space. The contents of his backpack are spread out on the surface, mixing lecture notes with dusty old tools and paint cans. A tightened bench vise holds up the business end of a music stand, displaying an American government textbook opened to an oddly-shaped map of the United States with each state drawn in proportion to its number of electoral votes.

At the opposite end of the basement, buried behind storage boxes belonging to Chas's dad, we find an out-of-place washroom jutting out from the otherwise rectangular foundation. Upon this discovery, it's immediately clear that we must use this space for some clandestine purpose. There's remarkably little discussion about the project, as if the concept were inherent—a numinous voice commanding us to build.

We start hauling in lumber, and within a couple of days we've constructed a door and vestibule around the threshold, secured by a padlock. Just to be safe, we slide a bookshelf in front of the door and pile it full of old *National Geographic* issues.

When our roommates ask about the noise, we say that we're building a bookshelf. The fact of the matter is, no one else can know about this, just the three of us—Warren, Spencer, and me. This way, it exists only in our world. But simply building the room is not enough. We have to put something inside of it. Otherwise it's just an empty room.

4

MAHAMANVANTARA

Spencer is staring out the window through his bird-ing binoculars, spying on the campus security station across the lawn. He says he's been watching them for weeks, not to mention following them around on his bicycle.

"They don't do much," he says. "Just a loop around campus every now and then."

His dorm room is littered with canvases, easels, and palettes.

Little gray kneaded-eraser sculptures are scattered everywhere—

A Bodhi leaf pressed to the mirror.

A fly agaric sprouting from the window sill.

A little gray lemur climbing up the bed post.

And a curious number of little gray penises.

Various drawings of songbirds and human anatomy are spread out on the desktop. One in particular catches my eye: a pencil sketch of a naked obese woman lying on her side, plopped on the paper like a glob of jelly.

Above it all, positioned on top of the dresser, a red clay sculpture-in-progress overlooks the cluttered landscape like a desert butte.

Recently Spencer devised a fake art project centered around the Audubon books, sort of a modern take on *Birds of America*. He pitched the idea to the art department, asking for permission to photograph the pages. Being an avid birder himself, as well as one of the university's most gifted art students, his story checked out, and he was granted access to the Rare Book Room.

A few days later, he was first escorted through a fortified door with a security keypad and then ushered around the museum by that same friendly, grandma-like librarian named Betty. For the greater part of an hour, she highlighted Transy's most prized possessions, focusing mostly on *Birds of America*.

Spencer spins around in his swivel chair and opens his laptop. Throughout the tour, he was allowed to snap photos on a digital camera. Scrolling through the files on his computer, the three of us marvel at the vivid, life-sized, 19th-century watercolors of American birds in their natural habitats. Some of the highlights include: a majestic barn owl perched on a tree limb high above a meandering river, calmly staring forward (as if looking directly at us) with a dead chipmunk dangling from its mouth; a brown buzzard swooping down on a defenseless rabbit, illustrated in the split second before its talons dig into the petrified prey; and of course

Audubon's famous American Flamingo, with its vibrant pink body and long, outstretched neck hunched over the water of a muggy lagoon. Although Spencer kind of kills the mood when he informs us that Audubon in fact shot and killed each bird before painting it.

To our surprise, Betty even gave Spencer permission to photograph other works unrelated to Audubon. Like *Hortus Sanitatis de Laten en Francois,* the first natural history encyclopedia, a two-volume Latin treatise on herbs, medicine, and natural history, with ornate woodcut illustrations, circa 1500, translated to French, and custom-made for King Henry VII and *Illuminated Manuscripts,* a devotional calendar decorated with fancy calligraphy and gold illuminations, written at Winchester in 1425. Not to mention, one that needs no introduction, a first-edition of Charles Darwin's *On the Origin of Species.*

Throughout the course of the tour, Spencer was able to glean other bits of useful information as well. For example, he learned that the staff elevator leads directly into the museum, and that there are no alarms attached to any of the pieces. However, an intricate after-hours security system pretty much rules out breaking in at night.

"But during the day, there's almost zero security— *no cameras, no alarms, nothing!* Everything is guarded by a little old lady, and all it takes is an appointment," Spencer says, as he casually closes his laptop and strolls out of the room to use the communal restroom down the hallway.

The moment he's gone, Warren shoots up from his chair and rushes over to the bookshelf. He slides out a notebook and shuffles through the pages, searching for a particular spot.

"You need to read this," he says, handing me the notebook. I've seen it before—it's Spencer's sketch pad from the Appalachian Trail.

"Hurry before he gets back!"

I skim over the page, struggling to decipher Spencer's tangled, chaotic words. The passage starts out normal enough, just mundane notes about the weather. Then it takes an unexpected turn:

> *I have decided that Warren and Eric are trying to kill me. Large outcroppings have interested them. Tomorrow I get out. Wake up and leave. Don't trust them. Trust your gut. Get out. Fast. They couldn't keep up with you if they tried. You must go and you must go fast. Get up early. Grab your food, leave. They could never catch you.*

I stare blankly across the room, struggling to make sense of what I've just read. One of Spencer's paintings is propped up against the wall—a landscape of abstract chaos, blurred lines and commotion, a world in disarray. If you stare long enough, eventually the dystopian wasteland fades away and the separate scenes come into focus. Suddenly the labyrinth appears less convoluted and lawless. Everyone is just going about their lives, focused on themselves, unaware of the whirlwind circling around them.

———

Crossing the atrium, we keep our heads down, eyes fixed on the polished limestone floor of the massive, brand-new, twenty million-dollar UK student library. Sunlight streaks across the marble from the skylight above.

Sponges.

Ammonites.

Belemnites.

Brachiopods.

Squiggles and doodles with geometric purpose.

Bright-white foraminifera in all their godlike glory.

The slabs were imported from Bavaria—no expenses spared, paid for by a wealthy alumni from the zombie fraternity—here now for us lordly apes to kill time on.

Students loaf in Bauhaus lounge chairs, hunched over cellphone screens with necks bent like macaroni, crammed into endless alcoves and stacked high on a half-dozen levels around a towering rotunda.

Blending into the crowd, we move up the main staircase to the mezzanine, searching floors until we find a computer outside the view of security cameras.

With the three of us squeezed into a cubicle, Warren—or rather, *Mr. Beckman*—logs into an email account and types to his man in Amsterdam:

> Dear Sir,
>
> When we last corresponded, you were interested in acquiring my *Birds of North America*. In addition, I now plan to offer more of my collection, including: *Hortus Sanitatis de Laten en Francois*, two volumes, 450 woodcut illustrations, Paris circa 1500; *Illuminated Manuscripts*, Devotional Calendar, England circa 1425; and, last but not least, a first-edition, *On the Origin of Species by Means of Natural Selection*, by Charles Darwin. I have attached files containing photographs of the aforementioned works. If interested, please notify me at your earliest convenience.
>
> W.B.

As the getaway driver, it's my responsibility to find a car, so I call a guy who owes me a favor. He's a fast-talking cokehead, tormented by odd tics and paranoias.

I find him in his usual spot at the horse track, crammed into a simulcast betting booth with multiple television screens displaying live feeds from other sites around the country. While eying a close finish at Pimlico, he anxiously taps the spikes of his golf shoes on the floor and twists up a stack of horse-statistics spreadsheets.

"Fuck!" he shouts as the results come in, beating the wad of papers against the table like a riding crop.

"I need to borrow a car," I say. "Something big, like an SUV."

"Why, you moving?"

"No, just moving some stuff."

"I want in," he says, without hesitation.

I remind him that he still owes me a lot of money.

A few months ago, I loaned him some cash to supposedly settle a gambling debt. He said he needed to square up with his bookie, otherwise something "very bad" would happen to him. Based on his demeanor, I got the impression that something "very bad" translated to something "very painful." But there's no way of telling which parts of his stories are true, *if any*. He borrows and steals from one person just to pay off another, as if his life were an endless Ponzi scheme.

Suddenly he starts twitching and talking rapidly. "I could've s-s-sworn I paid you back," he insists, dumbfounded.

But I don't buy it, especially since he's already trying to feed me excuses, each one more convoluted than the last. With great theatrics, he narrates a long and complex tale of an ill-fated night when the universe set out to get him. Apparently the all-knowing cosmos had nothing better to do than mess with his late-night binger at Solid Platinum, the fully-nude strip club off the interstate. Long story short, he claims to have lost his cell phone (along with my number) and didn't know how to reach me. This at least would explain why he answered my call. He probably didn't recognize my number, otherwise he would've just avoided me for as long as possible. Now I have to sit through the whole song and dance.

"I'll get you that money by tomorrow," he promises, but then immediately starts backtracking. "If not tomorrow, then by the end of the week—next week *at the latest!*"

I've seen this act so many times. He's just going through the motions. The routine is second-nature to him. The truth is, we both know that he's not going to pay me back, so I have to make use of him in other ways.

"Besides, there's nothing to be in on," I say. "I'm just moving some stuff."

"Sure, man, whatever you need!"

He says he'll be in touch, but I've learned to doubt everything that comes out of his mouth.

As a backup plan, I start researching how to hot-wire cars. Just a quick internet search provides plenty of information. It seems simple enough:

Step 1: Remove steering column cover.

Step 2: Locate battery wires (usually red, but colors vary by manufacturer).

Step 3: Strip battery wire insulation.

Step 4: Twist stripped battery-wire ends together.

Step 5: Connect ignition wire (probably brown) and battery wire.

Step 6: Strip starter wire (probably yellow).

Step 7: Touch stripped starter-wire ends to battery wire ends (should spark).

Step 8: Break steering lock, and drive!

For weeks, I roam the streets around Transy, trying to recall getaway scenes from popular heist movies while applying my own method of inductive reasoning. I figure an effective getaway route should follow backroads, with as few traffic stops as possible, allowing us to maintain high speeds while minimizing course deviation.

Somewhere around the halfway point between Transy and the house, the elegant, old-money neighborhoods surrounding campus abruptly change from Colonial Revival mansions with pristine gardens to shotgun shacks and broken sidewalks. It's here, at a sharp bend in the road, I discover an abandoned warehouse: the perfect drop spot.

Standing on the curb, I watch the getaway unfold in my head like a movie scene—

Speeding around the corner, I pull the car into a covered portico. Shielded from view, the three of us ditch our disguises for new clothes, tossing all the evidence into trash bags.

While the two of them are transporting the books and evidence bags into the building, I burn the fake temporary tag that was taped inside the window, kicking dirt and gravel over the ashes. Before taking off, I screw in the real license plate. This way if anyone caught our fake tag number fleeing the scene, it won't be an issue.

Meanwhile, Warren and Spencer will hang tight inside the abandoned warehouse, effectively separating the suspects, the loot, and the evidence from the getaway vehicle. Once I switch out the hot car for my own, I'll return to pick them up.

If the circumstances are too dicey for them to remain in the drop spot, they can stash the books and leave on foot. It's not ideal, but we can always come back later to retrieve the loot.

━━

Warren calls the Special Collections department from a pay phone outside a liquor store and schedules a tour of the Rare Book Room under the pseudonym Walter Beckman. Altering his voice, he speaks in a deep, robotic tone, like an automated voice message. It's hard not to laugh.

We do this a number of times over the course of a few weeks, calling from different pay phones around town. Sometimes, just to switch it up, we schedule by email, using fake accounts on computers at the UK library.

However, Mr. Beckman never shows up to any of his appointments.

Instead, the three of us wait downstairs in the Transy library, watching staff members to see if any personnel or security changes occur during museum tours. But it's just business as usual.

Lately, we've been spending nearly all of our free time at the library. Stationed in different sections, we hunch over books to make it look like we're studying. Before leaving the house, I always grab the largest tome from my bookshelf, which, at the moment, is *Ulysses*.

Sitting at a study table, I open the book to one of the many dog-eared pages and act like I'm cramming for an exam. . . .

> Reading two pages apiece of seven books every night, eh? I was young. You bowed to yourself in the mirror, stepping forward to

applause earnestly, striking face. Hurray for the God-damned idiot! Hray! No-one saw: tell no-one. Books you were going to write with letters for titles. Have you read his F? O yes, but I prefer Q. Yes, but W is wonderful. O yes, W. Remember your epiphanies on green oval leaves, deeply deep, copies to be sent if you died to all the great libraries of the world, including Alexandria? Someone was to read them there after a few thousand years, a mahamanvantara. Pico della Mirandola like. Ay, very like a whale. When one reads these strange pages of one long gone one feels that one is at one with one who once. . . .

I sketch layouts and jot down information, anything that seems even remotely useful. Most of it pertains to employees' work schedules and habits, like the days of the week they work, when they take their breaks, how aware of their surroundings they are, how often they venture upstairs to the Rare Book Room. . . .

Pretending to be a Transy student, I explore every inch of the library, pulling on every single door handle, sometimes the doors open up to employees-only areas, in which case, I quickly scamper off, muttering abrupt remarks like, "Sorry, just looking for the computer lab," before they can ask me any questions.

When it's time to leave, I use the opportunity to test emergency exit doors. They all read: *Emergency Exit — Do not enter — Alarm will sound.* If I'm caught, I'll just act oblivious, like I didn't see the bright-red warning sign directly in front of my face. I used to get really nervous when I approached the doors. It wasn't just the fear of setting off the alarm; it was much more than that, like stepping into the unknown, opening a door that can't be closed.

Except nothing ever happens—the alarm never sounds, no one even notices.

Instead, the door closes softly behind me, and I walk back home.

———

Sitting in Warren's living room, the three of us present new information we've collected. We used to meet once a week to work on the heist, but now it's almost every day.

Warren packs his bong, "Beelzebong," and starts recording the conversation on his tape recorder. With so much information lost in the fog of drugs, we try to record every session.

After deliberations, we vote on the issues. Key amendments require a majority decision. Depending on the outcome, we either discard an idea or incorporate it into the working plan.

It's strange how it all seems so normal now. The whole thing started as a game, like playing Cops and Robbers as a kid. The gun isn't real—it's just your finger. So, you string it along until it becomes an obsession, dancing and slithering in front of you like a Chinese dragon. *You want salvation?* it says. *You must destroy to create; you must suffer to be reborn.* The portal has always been there, staring back at you like distant memories . . . like Catholic grade school, crammed into a box with some fat, sweaty priest, confessing all the details of your prepubescent sins. *I confess to Almighty God, and to you, father, that I have sinned—I jerked off, father!* Ten Hail Mary's is your punishment. They say he speaks for God, and you believe them. Now look at what they've done to you. You're an idiot child, praying on your knees to some alien queen.

Lately I've been saying things that I don't entirely comprehend. The words just fall from my mouth as if they're someone else's. Oftentimes, it feels like I'm floating outside of my body, watching an actor play me on stage.

Actor Eric turns to Warren and Spencer: "Even if I knew that we were going to get caught," he says, "I'd still go through with the heist."

They stare at me, puzzled.

Desperately trying to change the subject, I propose that we come up with a code word for "abort mission," and I blurt out the first thing that comes to mind.

"How about, *Dixie's dead?*"

For example, I might call Warren or Spencer and say something like: *I am sorry to inform you that Dixie is dead. She was struck by a car. I'm terribly sorry. There was nothing we could do. Our sweet girl is gone, and she's never coming back.*

What this would really mean is: *Drop what you're doing—as in now, right now, this instant! Let go of whatever you're holding onto. Loosen your grip, and let it slip from your hand. It will fall and it will shatter—tiny pieces will spread thin—but something stronger will be rebuilt. Take a deep breath. You've prepared for this. About an hour's drive away is a cave beside a lake where the three of us once hiked. That's where we'll all meet up.*

Unless, of course, Dixie actually is dead, which is a scenario we've not yet prepared for.

In the corner, Spencer is busy at the workbench developing our disguises. Holding a hand mirror in front of himself, he carefully dabs makeup on his face. Though still in the early phases, Spencer insists that with a little prosthetics and artistry, he can transform us into old men.

"It has to look believable," he says. "If Betty peeks through the window and sees a couple of lunatics dressed up in Halloween costumes, she'll never let us inside."

"Which reminds me," Warren chimes in. "Our man in Amsterdam is *very much* interested in the additional pieces."

Based on Spencer's reaction—or rather, his lack thereof—I take it that I'm the last one to know, as usual.

"Everything is in place," Warren says, while messing around with his new stun gun.

"Actually, it's called a stun *pen*," he says. "The most nonlethal stun device on the market." He bought it at a nearby hunting supply store, which apparently sells self-defense weapons as well.

Warren says it's for intimidation, on the chance that Betty chooses not to cooperate with our plan. The loud crackling sound alone should be enough to keep her quiet.

Without warning, he presses the sparking device to my arm.

"God damn it, Warren!" I jump back, rubbing the spot where he shocked me. The jolt was sort of like the static-electric shock you get from touching a doorknob.

"I don't want to hurt you," Warren whispers in my ear. "I'm just here for the books."

He grabs my shoulder and lowers me down to the cold, concrete floor, zip-tying my arms and legs. He's hesitant at first. It takes some practice. So we repeat the process over and over. "I don't want to hurt you . . . I don't want to hurt you," Warren's voice echoes in my head, until I believe him.

With D-day fast approaching, I call my guy to arrange a time to pick up the getaway car, but he doesn't answer his cell phone.

After hours of nonstop calling, I head to the race track to look for him. Since he practically lives there, I figure I'm bound to run into him eventually, but he never turns up.

All night long, I drive around town casing his usual bars and shady gambling dens.

I sit in my car, watching people coming and going, but there's no sign of him anywhere. This goes on for days—me driving from one of his hangout spots to another, all the while leaving him vicious, hate-filled voicemail messages.

"You fucking conman . . . cocksucker! . . . no-good cokehead!" Most of the messages trail off with me trying to come up with other demeaning C-words.

Eventually, I just give up—it's useless. I already know exactly what he's going to do anyway. I've seen it many times before. He'll lay low for a while, like the cockroach that he is. Then, when I finally find him, he'll feed me some bullshit story. That's his thing, feeding people bullshit. He gets off on it.

Wait . . . cockroach . . . that's another C word!

I consider calling him back to use it, but it won't make a difference. We can't change our true natures. Besides, these creatures were here long before us, and will continue to survive after we are gone. In fact, they say in the event of nuclear annihilation, cockroaches will inherit the earth.

———

Back at the house, I break the news to Warren and Spencer that we don't have a getaway car. So, I propose we move to Plan B: Stealing a car.

But now, suddenly, they don't like the idea of grand theft auto.

"Too risky," Warren says. "Just one more thing to worry about."

Out of nowhere, he suggests that we bring in Chas.

"How is that a solution?" I ask.

"Chas is always into shady shit," Warren says. "Plus he's loaded, and we could use a money-man."

But I don't trust Chas. He's a deranged rich kid who's always getting into violent confrontations. Back in high school, he once tried to fight me at a house party because he said I looked at him the wrong way.

The fact that I'm actually living under the same roof as Chas is a testament to how badly I needed out of the fratboy-infested dorms. When I heard a room had opened up in the house, I quickly jumped on the opportunity. I thought that with just a little more time and space, I could find a way out of this mess.

———

The detached garage is split into two rooms. In the front, where cars would normally be, is a large party room consisting of a pool table, a ragged, albeit spacious, floral-patterned sectional sofa, and a home-made bar built from spare wood with the headboard of a bed as the countertop. Someone had the bright idea to paint the bordering fabric a shiny Kentucky blue; but the paint never quite dried, resulting in endless drunken college kids stumbling away from our house baffled by their newly-painted torsos.

In the back, previous owners converted a storage area into an opium den of sorts. It's a narrow, dimly lit room, with an assortment of tattered Rococo-style chairs on an Oriental rug, encircled by an unbroken wall mural of crudely painted demons.

Crammed into the corner, Chas rhythmically whirls his arms, while a nearly invisible speed-punching bag slams back and forth between the platform and his fists. An old ESPN *Jock Jams* album is playing on the boom box, blaring one of those overplayed pop songs you always hear at sporting events.

Standing in the doorway, the three of us watch him quietly, as if he were a foreign creature in his natural habitat. He tries to ignore us at first, but eventually gives up.

"Can I help you guys?" Chas shouts over the loud music, still pumping his fists.

We ask him to meet us in the basement when he's done.

A little while later, Chas grudgingly moseys down the staircase, wearing a black silk robe with his initials stitched into the chest pocket. Many of his belongings are marked this way, as it is customary in affluent Southern society for family members to bestow upon one another such gifts, usually in the form of tanned leather hide (flasks, belts, wallets, etc.) emblazoned with one's initials or family crest.

"Is this going to take long?" he asks, collapsing onto Warren's bright-orange, thrift store-lifted sofa chair. "My bath is getting cold."

Warren, the unofficial spokesman of the group, begins the conversation with Chas the same way he did with me, by demanding allegiance before anything else. A clever salesman, he has a way of getting you to sign up for things you know nothing about. For me, the heist was like a sword dangling over my head, as if rejecting Warren's proposal also meant the end of our friendship. Persuading Chas, on the other hand, would require a different approach.

"We've been working on something," Warren says. "It's big—the payout could be huge."

"How huge?" Chas responds.

Warren leans in close and whispers, *"Twelve million dollars."*

Chas instantly sits up straight in his chair.

"We'd like to bring you in on this," Warren adds, "but first we need to know that we can trust you."

"Of course you can trust me!" Chas insists, even though everyone knows that's a lie.

In fact, Chas is the one who'd floated the unsubstantiated rumor that Warren had stolen my money. Years ago, the two were close friends, but over time Warren started hanging out with other people, namely Spencer and me. Because of this, Chas resented Warren and seemed intent on ruining his life in any way possible.

Nevertheless, Warren starts revealing the details of the heist, starting from the beginning. To my surprise, he designates Chas as the new getaway driver, and for his first assignment, charges him with the task of finding an untraceable vehicle.

Although, at the moment, Chas's mind is somewhere else. Throughout the conversation, he continuously shakes his head in disbelief while repeating the phrase, "Twelve million dollars!"

Moments ago, he was ready to walk out of the room (after all, his bath is getting cold), but now he's utterly captivated. It seems that Warren hit the nail directly on the head: money is the only thing Chas cares about.

These days, I can hardly even look at him, as if one person could embody pure, unadulterated arrogance. To me, Chas represents an elitist Lexington crowd that I've grown to despise over the years. The moment I see his face, anger starts boiling up inside me, and I have to look away—that's the only way to stop it. If we were outside during daylight, I could just stare up at the sun, as I've found partial blindness to be the best remedy. Since that option is out of the question, however, I desperately scan the room for some sort of distraction.

One of Spencer's drawings, titled, *The Fruit Basket,* is framed and propped up on Warren's dresser like a family photo. It's a tasteful pencil sketch of penis and testicles smooshed together, tucked between legs, and viewed from behind.

I try to drown out the background noise—*"Twelve million dollars! Do you know what we could do with that kind of money?"*—by fixating on the lumpy goulash of genitalia. I remember the first time I saw it. At first, I couldn't figure out what I was looking at. I stared for a while, puzzled. Then suddenly it came into focus like a Magic Eye image. "Whoa!" I'd recoiled. "Whose junk is that?" To which Spencer replied, "Mirrors," with a wink.

———

With Mr. Beckman's appointment fast approaching, we're all rushing around to put the finishing touches on our plan. Unfortunately, most of my time is spent bringing Chas up to speed.

One day, while driving a test run, Chas mentions that he found the perfect getaway vehicle. His aunt is selling a used minivan to an out-of-state buyer, and the transaction is set to take place the day after the heist.

"As long as we have the van back beforehand, no one will even notice it was missing," Chas says. "By the next day, it will be in a completely different state with a completely different owner."

I hate to admit it, but it actually sounds like a pretty good plan.

On the day of the heist, we'll park the van outside of the library in the closest spot to the fire exit, and the four of us will walk inside together.

Since it's the day before winter break, the building should be nearly empty. Most of the students will have already finished their final exams and hightailed it out of campus.

No one will even notice when we enter the building, dressed up as old men, and walk calmly across the lobby. Employees and students alike, will just be going about their business, eager to get home for the holidays. That's when Warren, Spencer, and I will proceed up the staircase, while Chas waits behind as a lookout. Halfway up, I'll stop and hold my position, as they continue on to the second level. In front of the Rare Book Room, they'll be greeted by Betty, the lone curator. Standing out of sight, I'll hear the brief encounter before they enter the museum, at which point a heavy security door will close behind them.

Waiting nervously, I'll try to imagine the scene unfolding in an adjacent room, but the prospect is unthinkable. The whole thing still feels like a fantasy. Surely something will stop us, right?

What's taking so long? I'll wonder, until I hear the latch unbolting.

Peeking my head around the corner, I'll see Spencer holding the door open for me. That's when I'll give Chas the thumbs-up signal, which means that I'm heading upstairs to help Warren and Spencer bring down the books.

Chas will shoot back the same signal, meaning he received my message and will proceed accordingly, before exiting the building to prepare the van for our escape. If Chas would have responded with a thumbs-down signal, it would've indicated that the path was not clear, in which case we would hold the position until further notice. However, if he, or anyone else for that matter, were to make a throat-slashing motion, it would mean to abort the mission completely.

A couple minutes later, the three of us will emerge from the staff elevator on the main level, carrying the large Audubon manuscripts wrapped in sheets for concealment, with the remainder of the books loaded in our backpacks. We'll skirt the edge of the lobby, momentarily in plain view, before reaching the staircase to the fire exit.

Outside, Chas will be waiting for us in the driver's seat of the van, the doors already opened. We'll hop inside and casually drive out of the parking lot, following our established getaway route.

Everything will go smoothly.

That's the plan, at least.

5
THE DAY OF

Spencer leans in close and smears a dab of makeup on my forehead. He's wearing a brown tweed suit and a gray wig, with foundation and prosthetics covering his face. I can't stop staring at his gnarled, latex nose. *I hope mine looks better than that,* I think to myself, only to recall that he actually has to go inside the museum and interact with Betty, face-to-face.

On the other side of the room, Warren is similarly disguised in a gray suit, with a wig and flatcap on his head. He's bent over the coffee table, wiping his weird-looking face up and down the surface, snorting lines of coke up his goblin-like nose-holes.

"We just have to do it," he says to no one in particular, sniffing and wiping his nose. "We just have to force ourselves!"

The sight of this should probably disturb me more than it does, but I guess deep down I've always known that we would end up here. At least I can take comfort in the fact that, one way or another, it will all be over with today.

It's not long before Chas arrives with the van, and the three of us pile inside. While he's unscrewing the license plate, I tape the fake temporary tag to the inside of the rear window, just as we've practiced many times before. We go through the motions like passive robots, each performing our own particular function. That's the only way to get through it, by detaching yourself from reality and hoping that repetition carries you through.

No one says a word for the entire drive over to Transy.

I close my eyes and envision the heist unfolding the way we planned it, as if by focusing hard enough my thoughts could manifest into reality.

As we pull off the main road, Chas mutters under his breath, "Shit."

I open my eyes to see that the parking lot is full of cars, forcing us to park on the very opposite side, in one of the farthest possible spots from the library.

Why is it so crowded? Shouldn't everyone be gone by now?

But there's no time to think about it.

"It's not a deal-breaker," Warren says. "Just stick to the plan."

The four of us quietly exit the van and walk two-by-two across the lawn toward the library. I try to control my breathing and stay alert, but it feels like it's taking forever to reach the entrance.

When we finally start up the front steps, a student politely holds open the door for what, at first glance, appears to be a group of elderly men out for an afternoon stroll.

I hadn't truly considered how ridiculous we might appear up close until I see the look on the young man's face: a silent, unblinking stare of confusion. He must assume it's some sort of prank, and he starts to smile—the corner of his lip curling up ever slightly—but he's not certain. As we inch closer, he begins having second thoughts, and his half-smile fades. *Should I do something . . . say something?* he's clearly asking himself. Unable to decide, the young man ends up somewhere in between, gawking awkwardly as we slide past him into the library.

We cross the lobby, and I try not to make eye contact with anyone, but it's difficult with people whispering and pointing at us.

Students cramming for final exams peer up from their textbooks, assuming they are witnessing some sort of end-of-the-semester prank, or worse, a performance art piece. Their eyes follow us around the library, waiting for the show to start.

At the staircase, Chas remains behind, just as we planned. Halfway up, I stop and hold position, while Warren and Spencer continue. But moments later they return, walking back down the stairs toward me.

Confused, I join them.

"What's going on?" I whisper.

Once Chas is in earshot, Warren explains that there are two women waiting at the reception desk, and neither one of them is Betty. Since it goes against everything we have planned, Warren and Spencer immediately turned around.

The four of us are whispering to each other at the base of the staircase, debating about what to do next.

"Who were they?"

"Where the fuck is Betty?"

"What should we do?"

Meanwhile, giggling spectators are gathering nearby, waiting for us to do something, so we retreat downstairs to the basement and hide out in an empty study room.

"Fuck it!" Warren says. "Let's just do it!"

But it's a major deviation from the plan. Instead of just dealing with Betty, they would have to subdue two other strangers, and that's not something anyone feels comfortable with. There are too many unknown factors.

Eager to get out of the building, we quickly climb the staircase. At the top, a handful of students are waiting for us.

All I can think about is running. It doesn't even matter where to, just far away from here. Then I remember that I haven't actually done anything illegal, which instantly puts my fears to rest. As far as they know, we are just some dudes walking around in costumes.

Just inside the exit, I pass a group of wide-eyed students. Hoping to ease the tension, I tip my hat and say,

"Good day!" As I'm waltzing out the door, I can hear them laughing.

We drive home in silence. Again, no one says a word, except this time, it's for a different reason. We spent so much time conceptualizing the heist that the thought of throwing in the towel never even seemed like an option.

It was all downhill from the start.

First off, the place was packed, and just to make matters worse, all the good parking spots were taken.

Then, our disguises were a complete failure. We couldn't even get past the bystanders, which means that Warren and Spencer never would have fooled Betty (who was nowhere to be found, anyway). Although, her sudden disappearance may have saved us from a complete disaster.

Sure, we were all relieved to walk back out of the library, into the sunshine, without having committed a major felony. But, there will always be a lingering sense of obligation, like we won't be able to live with ourselves for not going through with it. Now it feels like we are stuck somewhere in between, with nowhere to go.

Back at the house, everyone goes their separate way without speaking.

I wander around campus for a while before bombing a Geography exam. All I could remember was a documentary we watched in class about the archaic practice of foot binding, conjuring up grotesque images of mangled Asian women's feet, which served no purpose on the exam. I guess I shouldn't be surprised, though. It's not like I've been to class much lately. With everything that's been going on, the prerequisites seem even more pointless than before. Really, the only reason I'm even taking finals is to keep up appearances. This way, if we're ever questioned about the heist, we can try to create an alibi.

Who . . . me? You think I was involved in what? A rare book heist? At Transy? During finals week? You can't be serious! This must be a mistake. Ask my roommates, they'll tell you. I've just been studying and taking exams—my professors will confirm that. A book heist . . . at Transy? During finals week?

Outside of the classroom building, I sit on a bench in the quad and stare at an old, severed tree trunk embedded in cement and cordoned off by a post-and-chain fence. Swarms of students rush in and out of the building, mindlessly skirting the landmark. Like everyone else, I pass the spot every day without even giving it a second thought. Now I come to find out that it's actually the oldest thing on campus.

Nearby, an easy-to-miss sign chronicles the tree's history, replete with a diagram titled, "Stages in the Development and Finding of the Stump," using terms like "swamp muck" and "shaly sandstone" to depict the many stages of the stump's long and fateful demise:

The Whitfield Stump

The fossil is the preserved stump and root system of a lycopod tree that lived approximately three hundred million (300,000,000) years ago in a swampy forest in what is now Harlan County, Kentucky. The base of this tree was buried several feet deep in mud during a flood and the tree died. The mud covering the roots and stump hardened slowly in the next few years while the tree rotted away. The pithy wood rotted and its place was taken by more mud which washed in at the top of the stump. The tough bark did not rot completely and eventually turned to coal. The stump as we now see it is not "petrified wood" but sandstone that faithfully preserves the shape of the old trunk and major roots.

Apparently the stump was discovered in the 1930's when it fell from the roof of a coal mine in Harlan, Kentucky, an impoverished Appalachian city in the southeastern corner of the state along the Virginia border. Back in elementary school, we used to hold canned-food drives specifically for the residents of Harlan—that's how bad it was there. Teachers would tell us dreadful stories of poor, hungry children who weren't fortunate enough to eat dinosaur-shaped chicken nuggets like we were. Over time, in my young mind, Harlan became a hellish netherworld where barefoot mountain kids foraged through the forest on hands and knees, begging God for the life-giving sustenance of Campbell's Cream of Mushroom soup.

The tree's story goes on to describe how the manager of the coal mine widened the passageway and even built a special car to remove the massive stump. Afterward, he cemented the roots and put it on display. It's not clear when, but at some point he donated the artifact to the university. At the bottom of the inscription, a footnote adds that a pamphlet containing more data can be obtained from the librarian in the Geology Department Library. For a moment, I actually consider heading over there to check it out. It's only about a ten minute walk. But, on second thought, I think I've had enough of university libraries for today.

Still, I'm reluctant to head back home. I just need to be away from them for a while—away from all of that. I drive aimlessly around town until the sun goes down. Before long, I find myself trapped in bumper-to-bumper Christmas shopping traffic, a river of red and white beams steadily careening toward various shopping malls. Eventually the current pulls me into a busy parking lot where I stare blankly out the window, chain-smoking cigarettes, while hordes of families file into department stores like they've been given marching orders. The only other establishment

I've seen them flock so earnestly to is church, which, much like the shopping mall, is on just about every other corner.

Without thinking, I end up driving to my parents' house, on the outskirts of town, where I grew up. Parked out front, I turn off the engine and stare into the dark. There are no streetlights out here, just gradients of black. It's actually kind of soothing at first. I can't remember the last time I felt so hidden. But it doesn't last long, as my mind concedes to paranoia, fixated on the prospect of zombies lurking in the shadows.

What am I doing here? I ask myself.

Just as I'm about to leave, the garage light turns on, and my mom pops her head out the side door. She squints for a second then rushes over to the car, doing one of those rigid, winter shimmies suddenly induced by venturing outside without a coat.

"Brrr!" she says, cracking open the door and rubbing her hands up and down her arms for warmth. "Is everything okay?"

Seeing how I just showed up unannounced, she presumes that something must be wrong—and understandably so, since I haven't really kept in touch lately, and I come around the house even less.

Every other week, she tries to make contact with me, but I'm usually too drunk or high to speak coherent sentences.

Don't answer the phone, I tell myself. *It would be a disaster. I'd only sound deranged.*

I let the call go to voicemail.

I'll text her back later. It's better this way for everyone.

Finally, after a long and taxing mental debate, I'll compose a proper text—or rather, what I think a proper person would say in such a situation, full of all the appropriate pleasantries. Just a normal boy texting his mother.

But then I start second-guessing myself.

This isn't how normal people talk, is it?

I'll delete the text and start writing a new one, only to delete that and end up back on the first one, before deleting that one again.

I'll come back to this later with a fresh perspective, I tell myself.

But inevitably I pass out.

The next day, I'll notice the text again and remember that I never responded.

Now it's been too long, I think, as if that makes sense.

This is how I rationalize not speaking to my own mother, the one who brought me into this world.

"I was just in the neighborhood," I say.

It's such an absurd line. Not only is it word-for-word the exact phrase that every movie character repeats when lying about their true intention for showing up somewhere unannounced, but it's also clearly not true. I would never *just be in the neighborhood.* There's nothing out here except for churches and horse farms.

"Okay . . . ," she says, shivering and confused. "You staying for dinner?"

The moment I set foot inside the house, my sister is immediately on my case. "I hear you were just in the neighborhood," she says, with a suspicious tone.

A sophomore in high school, she's going through that sassy, know-it-all phase. But I know she's just worried about me, like everyone else in my family. I can tell by the way they look at me, like they know that something's wrong but can't quite figure out what it is. I can only imagine what they say about me when I'm not around.

It's gotten worse since he left for college.

He seems angry now.

What's with all the cuts and bruises?

I think he's on drugs.

To be fair, none of these observations would be incorrect.

A little while later, my older brother walks through the door. Mom must have invited him over for dinner when she found out I was staying, wasting no time jumping at the opportunity. Despite the fact that everyone lives within a ten-mile radius, these days it's rare for all five of us to be together under one roof.

When I was growing up, my parents always made a big deal about eating dinner together, as if it were a sacred ritual. Back then, the etiquette was more strict. Before eating, the television had to be turned off, and everyone participated in communal prayer thanking God for the food we were about to eat. But over the years, the decorum has eased. After 9/11, I stopped praying, and the television stayed on.

We bow our heads as my parents quickly recite a prayer like they're retelling a story and rushing through the frivolous parts—

Bless us, O Lord, and these thy gifts . . . yada yada yada . . . Amen. Let's eat!

This is the part where everyone's supposed to talk about their days. As usual, I don't have much to share.

My mom, a kindergarten teacher, complains about a rowdy addition to her classroom. "I mean, this kid is out of control!" she says, laughing despairingly to herself. "Honestly, I don't know what I'm going to do."

Meanwhile, my dad is staring across the room at the television screen, watching the national news— another nightly ritual. He didn't hear anything my mom just said because he was focused on the TV. Every now and then he nods and mumbles something like, "Oh yeah?"

In my father's defense, the nation is in turmoil. As the news anchor reports, Dick Clark was hospitalized after suffering a stroke and will not be able to host his traditional New Year's Eve television special. But that's not even the upsetting part—it's that Regis Philbin is rumored to be taking his place.

After repeating the joke a couple of times in my head, I give it a test run on the table, but I only manage to get a snicker out of my brother.

As everyone passes around plates of meat and vegetables, I try to imagine how different the scene would look if I'd been arrested earlier today for attempted robbery.

"Why'd he do it?" my sister would ask between sobbing gasps, making one of those horrible, scrunched-up cry-faces. (Even in this hypothetical scenario, I can't help but wince at the sight.)

My brother urges everyone to stay calm until they know more information. He wraps his arm around my sister, an unusual gesture in our family. We've never been big touchers, never really said *I love you* to one another, although I think it was always implied.

Meanwhile, my parents are standing over the table, scouring the yellow pages for criminal defense attorneys. Mom suggests calling her old friend from back home. You know, the mythical lady with the fucked-up son who supposedly got into a bunch of trouble once?

"It was probably just a prank," my dad says. "I bet it was that fricking fraternity!" Full disclosure: I never told my family I quit the frat. "Those jackasses are always pulling these sorts of stunts!"

Who knows? Maybe this is a second chance.

—

Back at the house, I find everyone waiting for me in the basement.

"Where have you been?" Warren asks, clearly annoyed.

"I went home for dinner."

"We've been calling you!" Chas snaps.

Earlier in the evening, I needed to disconnect for a little while, so I turned off my cell phone. I couldn't imagine why they would need to reach me. After all, the heist is over—*we failed!* What else is there to talk about?

"I emailed Betty," Warren says. "I wanted to apologize for missing the appointment. But get this, apparently she missed it too—*a personal matter,* or something. Can you believe that?"

They're all just sitting there, staring, waiting for me to say something.

"Her coworkers filled in for her," he adds, excitedly. "That's who those women were!"

"All right . . . ," I say, turning back up the staircase. "Glad we cleared that up."

"So I rescheduled the appointment for tomorrow," Warren blurts out.

"What?"

"Betty was able to squeeze us in," he says, grinning. "It's our last chance before everything shuts down for winter break."

"Are you serious?"

"We are going to do things a little differently this time, though," Warren explains, while Spencer and Chas nod their heads in agreement. "We're ditching the costumes. Obviously, they didn't fool anyone. We'll just bundle up in winter clothes. We figure that Betty has never seen us before, so she won't be able to identify us. It'll all be over with before she even knows what's happening."

"Seeing how it went so smoothly last time," I mutter.

"The only thing is," Warren says, glancing over at the other two, "without the disguises, Spencer can't be anywhere near the library, or he could be identified. Which means that you'll have to come inside with me."

"What do you mean by 'come inside?'"

"I mean that you'll have to rob the museum with me," he says.

"That's what I thought you were going to say."

"Chas will stay in the van—no need for him to come inside," Warren says, casually brushing over the details. "He'll be parked outside the fire exit. This way we can just jump into the van and take off."

"Yeah . . . it's just that, I don't think I can tie some-one up."

"We're not going to hurt anyone!" Warren says. "You're overthinking it! We're just going for the books—that's all! We'll be in and out. Afterward, we'll place an anonymous phone call to the library to let them know she's up there. All right?"

But it's all a little overwhelming. Just moments ago, I was mulling over the details of my return to normal crime-free life. Now, I'm suddenly back in the mix, with a heavy new burden to boot.

I try to picture myself doing it—grabbing the old woman by her arm, forcing her to the ground, binding her limbs—but I just can't. It feels like a wall is standing in my way, and whatever lies on the other side is off-limits.

When I was young, my family's local grocery store was robbed at gunpoint. The thieves forced everyone into an office and tied them up. As a child, hearing about the crime completely unnerved me. Before the incident, it hadn't occurred to me that these sorts of things could just happen to innocent people, in broad daylight no less. From that point on, whenever my mom went to the store, I would always volunteer to go with her. She thought it was cute, like I wanted to spend more time with her—she called me her "little helper"—not realizing that I was actually there to protect her. *What happens to boys as they get older that turns them into animals?* I wondered, while floating down frozen-food aisles and eying suspicious customers from the prow of the shopping cart like a figurehead, as my mother captained the ship.

"Yeah," I say, exhaling loudly and shaking my head. "I just don't think I can do it."

Judging by everyone's reactions, they're clearly annoyed with my response, but I don't know what else to say. Before, when I was just a lookout, I'd somehow justified the harsher aspects of the robbery simply because I wouldn't physically be inside the room as it was taking place. Now I'm being asked to do the one thing that I've always said I wouldn't do.

"Fine," Warren blurts out. "I'll do it myself!"

"What do you mean?"

He thinks quietly to himself, still working out all the details in his head. After a long pause, he turns to me and says, "Okay, how about this? I show up to the appointment alone. You stay downstairs in the library—just act like you're studying or something. Once Betty is, um, taken care of, I'll call your phone and let you inside. Then we just load up the books and take off. That's all you have to do. You won't even see her!"

"And you're okay with doing that on your own?" I ask.

"Sure," he shrugs. "I'll be fine."

With no other objections, we spend the rest of the night hashing out the details of the new plan. Tomorrow is the last day of the semester before winter break. The minivan, our getaway vehicle, is being picked up by its new owner in the early afternoon. For all intents and purposes, this is our last shot. Surprisingly, everyone seems rejuvenated, as if this will set straight our colossal failure from this morning.

I guess this is my second chance after all.

6

SECOND CHANCE

In the morning, we pile back into the van, this time minus one. Chas is driving, while Warren's in the passenger seat talking to Spencer on a cell phone that I've never seen before. Earlier, when I asked him about it, he replied that he'd nabbed it off some kid on campus. After that, I didn't push him for any more details.

Spencer, our lookout, is positioned in the top-floor window of a building across the street from the library, equipped with his birding binoculars. If anything goes wrong, he'll be our eyes and ears.

The three of us are dressed in multiple layers of winter clothes—hats, jackets, scarves—anything to alter our appearances. Plus we've each added our own little finishing touches. For example, I usually wear contact lenses, so today I wore my glasses; and since I always have a beard, I shaved my face down to the skin.

Warren, on the other hand, got up early this morning and bleached his hair blond. After the heist, he'll immediately dye it back to its original color, brown.

This way, only witnesses to the crime will have seen him with blond hair.

"We're a couple minutes out," Warren says into the phone, loud enough for everyone to hear. *"Get ready."*

The moment we turn off the main road, into Transy's long U-shaped parking lot, I can tell that things are completely different from the day before. The majority of the spaces are empty, most importantly the ones closest to the fire exit.

Wasting no time, Chas whips the van into the spot and parks it.

They both turn around and stare at me.

I expected there to be more of a hassle, like the day before, but so far everything is going smoothly.

"Okay," I say, taking a deep breath. "Here we go, I guess."

"See you on the other side," Warren says, somewhat ominously.

"Good luck," Chas blurts out, as I close the door behind me.

One step at a time, I tell myself, while walking up the stairs to the library entrance. It's hard to believe that I'm back in the exact same spot as yesterday, after everything that happened. For some reason, I just can't stop myself.

Once inside, I make my way across the lobby, brushing past a group of students, while simultaneously shielding my face from the employees at the front desk. No one seems to recognize me—*not that I really expected them to*—but I'd be lying if I said it wasn't in the back of my mind.

In a corner of the library, I find the perfect spot—a private, empty study room with a window overlooking the staircase leading up to the museum.

I quickly take a seat at the table, whip out *Ulysses* from my backpack, and open the book to its usual spot:

> Reading two pages apiece of seven books every night, eh?

I scan the library—what I can see of it, at least.

> I was young.

There are still a few stragglers doing some last-minute cramming, but it's nowhere near as crowded as yesterday. With just a few hours left before the semester ends, surely the only thing on everyone's mind is getting home for the holiday break. The last thing anyone would expect is a robbery.

> You bowed to yourself in the mirror, stepping forward to applause earnestly, striking face.

Just then I see Warren stroll past the study room window. We make eye contact but he doesn't acknowledge me, not even slightly, as if we were strangers. He looks completely different, and it's not just the bleached-blond hair. His demeanor, the way he carries himself, it's all foreign to me. Watching him ascend the staircase, I realize that I don't know this person, this alter ego who dabbles in fake passports and colludes with black-market art dealers in Amsterdam cafes. Then it suddenly occurs to me that I've just witnessed the transformation into Walter Beckman, as Warren recedes from view.

Hurray for the God-damned idiot! Hray!

My heart races uncontrollably. *Just stick to the plan*, I tell myself, turning back to the book. But I can't concentrate; my mind is all over the place. I end up scanning the same line over and over:

No-one saw: tell no-one.

Trying to keep my composure, I run down a checklist of objectives, like an actor nervously rehearsing his lines before taking the stage.

When Warren calls, I'll calmly exit the room and walk upstairs, where he'll be waiting for me with the door open.

From there, I'll just head straight for the books. Warren—I mean, Mr. Beckman—should already have them out of their cases and ready to go.

Don't look at Betty! There's no need for that. It won't do any good. Try not to think about her. She'll be fine. Just act like she's not even there.

All you have to do is load up the books and get to the elevator.

Books, elevator . . . books, elevator . . . books, elevator.

What's taking so long? I wonder. *More unforeseen problems, like yesterday?*

I try to imagine what's going on up there, but really there's no telling. Any number of things could be taking place. For a second, I think I hear something—a faint thud on the ceiling—but it's probably just my imagination. Besides, let's be honest, this thing is probably never going to happen anyway. I mean, who are we kidding? We've been living in a fantasy world, delaying the inevitable anticlimactic end. Soon, I'll see Warren walking back down the stairs, disgruntled and shaking his head, and that's when I'll know it's finally over. Then we'll all go back to living our normal lives as if this never even happened.

No-one saw: tell no-one.

Years from now, when we're all fat and married and living in the suburbs, we'll tailgate together at college football games on the weekend. Every now and then someone will bring it up, usually when they've had too much to drink. "Remember that time we almost robbed a museum?" they'll whisper. We'll all laugh about it while peeking over our shoulders to make sure no one else is listening, always wondering what would have happened if we'd actually gone through with it, and how our lives would've been different.

Suddenly my phone starts buzzing. It's a number I've never seen before—presumably Warren's mysterious new cell phone—so I quickly answer the call.

"Hey buddy," Warren says. "Want to come on up?"

"Sure," I reply, warily. "Is everything . . . okay?"

"Yup," he says, cutting the conversation short. "Just come on up."

I try to walk calmly, but my legs are shaky from all the nerves and adrenaline—

One foot in front of the other.

Calm down!

It's not like we're walking into a robbery or anything.

We are just helping Warren—fuck, Walter!—carry some books down to the van. That's all—no big deal! Just go straight for the books and get to the elevator.

Books, elevator . . . books, elevator . . . books, elevator.

When I reach the top of the staircase, I freeze in my tracks, unable to process what I'm looking at—

Betty is standing there, holding the door open for me.

Countless panicked thoughts run through my mind at once—

This doesn't make sense.

What am I supposed to do?

Are we still going through with it?

"Mister Beckman tells me you're an Audubon admirer as well," Betty says, smiling and holding out her hand to greet me.

I keep my leather gloves on while shaking hands, which she clearly notices. But there's no telling what

Warren has planned, if anything, so I still need to be careful.

Betty instructs me to sign into the guest book before entering the museum, and immediately my mind goes blank. I hadn't prepared for this. Stalling for time, I act like I can't find the pen, but she quickly points out that it's directly in front of my face. The only name I can think of is a pseudonym we used to print on fake IDs: Harry Ballsagna. But obviously I can't write that, so I just scribble something down.

Betty leans in close and squints at what I've written.

"John Rutherford," she reads aloud, seemingly surprised.

I have no idea where it came from.

"Walter Beckman and John Rutherford!" Betty laughs, remarking that we both have doctor's names, whatever that means.

Smiling awkwardly, I look away and try not to make eye contact. I told myself that I wouldn't have to look at her. That's the only reason I agreed to this in the first place. Yet here we are, standing face-to-face in uncomfortable silence.

"Okay," Betty says, sensing my discomfort. "Let's start the tour!"

She leads us through a large, wood-carved double-door, with Warren on her heels.

I linger behind, unsure of what to do.

Are we just taking a tour now?

What's happening?

What are we doing?

I consider leaving while they're not looking.

Then, from the other side of the threshold, Warren shoots me an ominous glare. At first, I don't know how to interpret it, but that quickly changes as he wraps his arm around Betty and whispers something in her ear.

Oh fuck, it's happening!

I rush into the museum and pull closed the thick wooden doors in hopes of containing the situation.

As I turn back around, Betty lets out a bloodcurdling scream—

It rattles something loose in me, something I know I'll never get back.

Suddenly I'm outside of my body, paralyzed, watching the scene unfold.

Warren forces Betty down to the ground and tells her to be quiet.

"Help!" she cries out.

"We don't want to hurt you!" Warren pleads. "We're just here for the books."

He shouts something at me over and over, but I can't tell what he's saying. His voice sounds distant and muffled. I try to fight through the fog, clinging to his words like a lifeline pulling me back to the surface.

"Tie . . . up . . . her . . . feet!"

But I'm still just standing there, staring at him.

What is he talking about? Why would I do that? Her feet?

"In your bag!" he yells.

Then I remember that Warren slipped a bunch of zip ties into my backpack before we left the house. *Just in case,* he said. *You never know.* I didn't think much about it at the time. It just seemed like he was being thorough. But now, in retrospect, it all makes perfect sense.

Regardless, I don't have time to reflect on it now. There are more pressing issues at hand. Just because I wasn't supposed to be inside the room while the incident was taking place doesn't mean I'm any less culpable. Whether I like it or not, I'm a part of this. I helped create it. Besides, I've already crossed the line. There's no going back now.

I slide off my backpack and frantically rummage through the pockets until I find the zip ties.

Warren kneels down on the ground, struggling to get Betty's hands tied. When I try to pass him the ties, he shoots me an aggravated look.

"Put them around her feet!" he snaps.

As I approach Betty, she begs me not to hurt her, which takes me by surprise. *Of course I'm not going to hurt her,* I think. *That's ridiculous!* But she doesn't know that. She doesn't know anything about me. To her, I'm a monster capable of unspeakable cruelty. And as I'm cinching the zip ties around her ankles, that's exactly what I feel like—a monster.

Once Betty's feet are bound, I leave her behind with Warren and start searching for the Audubons.

Everything was supposed to be laid out in advance, per Mr. Beckman's request, but I only see the smaller items.

On the other side of the room, Warren props Betty up against the leg of a table.

"Please don't hurt me," she pleads with him.

"We have no reason to hurt you," Warren assures her. "We're just here for the books. It'll all be over soon."

With Betty out of the way, Warren rushes over to a display cabinet and slides open the drawers. Inside, the massive, four-volume *Birds of America* set is housed in its own special case, with each book measuring over 3 feet tall and 2 feet wide, and weighing around 50 pounds.

I quickly pull out the bed sheet from my backpack and unfold it on the floor. One at a time, we stack the giant folios in the center of the sheet, wrapping them up like a present—a twelve-million-dollar present. This way, if anyone sees us leaving the building, they'll just think that we're moving something bulky, and not necessarily the university's most prized possession. It may still look suspicious, but not *call-the-cops suspicious,* which is the only kind of suspicious we are concerned about.

With the Audubons ready to go, we move on to the smaller manuscripts, which are spread out neatly on the table. Prior to the appointment, Mr. Beckman asked that they be removed from their cases in advance to facilitate the viewing process. Dividing the pile between us, we quickly stuff the books inside our backpacks while trying not to damage the exteriors.

Before leaving, Warren and I take one last look around the room to make sure we didn't miss anything. I can't believe it's already over. It feels like there should be more to it, like we're forgetting something.

We hoist the Audubons from opposite ends. Together as a set, the four volumes are much heavier than we anticipated. There's no shortage of jostling and panicked remarks—

Hold on.

Just a sec.

Losing my grip over here.

Once inside the elevator, we rest the heavy load on our thighs and try to catch our breaths. Wasting no time, Warren pushes the button to the main level, and the elevator door closes.

"Here we go," he says, breathing deeply, like a soldier ready to charge into battle.

In the few moments remaining, I try to psych myself up for what is coming next. There's no telling what will be waiting for us on the other side of the door.

"Whatever it takes," I say. "Just get to the van."

When the elevator door opens, a woman walking past glances up from a clipboard and stops dead in her tracks. She stares at us for a moment, confused. It doesn't take long for her to put the pieces together. By the looks of it, she's definitely an employee and knows good and well that the two of us should not be inside the staff elevator, coming from the Rare Book Room, carrying large items wrapped in bed sheets.

"Stop!" the woman shouts, while moving toward us with her hand out.

Warren frantically hits the button to the basement level, and the door closes just before she reaches us.

Fortunately, when the door slides back open in the basement, there's no one waiting for us on the other side. However, there's also no exit down here either. So, no matter what, we'll have to get back up to the main level.

We set the books down for a moment to catch our breaths, blocking the elevator door from closing. Breathing heavily and doubled over, I stare down the hallway, waiting to see if anyone comes down the staircase looking for us, but no one does. The employee who spotted us must have rushed upstairs to the museum, which means that we need to get out of the building as soon as possible.

After a quick discussion, we decide to ride the elevator back up to the main level, where we first encountered the woman. By now she should be gone, either upstairs attending to Betty, or heading down here to look for us (the only other place we could be). Regardless, it's our only shot, and our window of escape is rapidly closing.

As the elevator starts moving, I try to psych myself up again. But now that we've been spotted, it's even more nerve-racking than before. *No matter what,* I tell myself. *Don't stop moving.*

When the door slides opens, no one is there.

Straining under the weight of the books, we rush out of the elevator, briefly skirting the lobby before turning the corner to the fire-exit stairwell. Struggling to keep the stack level, I crouch low, performing an awkward duck-walk while Warren hesitantly shuffles backward down the stairs. My biceps are burning, but I try to put the pain out of my mind.

One step at a time.

Just get to the van.

Don't stop moving.

The moment we reach ground level, someone lets out a piercing scream from the top of the staircase.

"What the hell are you doing?" she shouts.

It's the woman who spotted us in the elevator—she's tracked us down.

We're all frozen, staring at each other, waiting to see who makes the next move.

Suddenly, she barrels down the stairs toward us, screaming, "They're stealing the books!"

Out of options (other than a physical confrontation), we are forced to drop the books. I stand there, clenching my fists, anxiously bracing for impact, when all of a sudden Warren pulls me out the door—

Instantly, we're outside in the bright morning sunlight running frantically along the side of the building with a relentless middle-aged woman on our heels.

Up ahead, I see Chas scrambling to get the van ready, caught off guard by our frantic escape. He quickly slides open the side door for us, and then jumps into the driver's seat.

We dive inside the minivan and Chas instantly reverses out of the parking spot, nearly running over the woman in the process. She screams hysterically while pounding her palms on the back window.

As we peel out, the tires screech, capturing the attention of nearby pedestrians. Speeding through the parking lot, I wrestle with the sliding-door handle, finally getting it to shut when Chas slams on the brakes, before wildly cutting into traffic on North Broadway.

Right away, we turn down a two-lane road, speeding around cars, swerving in and out of oncoming traffic, narrowly missing an approaching sedan at one point.

Warren moves up front to the passenger seat to help Chas navigate. At least that's what I thought until he rolls down the window and sticks his head outside. Convulsing, he coughs up soup-bowl sized portions of vomit. With each heaving discharge, the yellow-orange mush catches wind and drivels down the side window in long streaks of what appears to have been a breakfast combo of oatmeal and orange juice.

As we speed through the stop sign at a four-way intersection, I grip the handle tightly and prepare for a head-on collision. Though somehow, time after time, we narrowly escape disaster, as if it were a scripted movie scene. Nothing about this world feels real anymore. The cars swerve just the right way, at just the right time—the choreography is flawless.

Still, my mind keeps going back to the library. All I can think about is how we left behind the Audubons, and that it was all for nothing.

"Fuck!" I yell, slamming my fist down onto the seat cushion.

"What?" Chas says, jerking the steering wheel back and forth, weaving through traffic. "What's wrong?"

"We didn't get them!" I say.

"You didn't get anything?" he shouts, infuriated at the thought of walking away empty-handed.

"We had to drop them."

Just then Warren pulls his head back inside the window and wipes the leftover vomit from his mouth. "Backpacks," he says, out of breath. "We got the backpacks."

I was so focused on the Audubons—not to mention, flustered by our frantic escape—that I'd completely forgotten about the backpacks, or for that matter, that I was even wearing one. I slide it off and take a quick inventory of the contents: *Origin of Species* and both volumes of *Hortus Sanitatis*. Meanwhile, Warren rummages through his pack and checks the remainder of the items off the list: *Illuminated Manuscripts* and Audubon's pencil sketches for *Birds of America,* along with an autographed synopsis. Even though we didn't get the pièce de résistance—the *Birds of America* set—there's still about one-million dollars' worth of rare manuscripts in our backpacks.

Moments later, Chas makes a sharp right turn and parks the van in the portico of the abandoned warehouse, shielding us from view of the street.

Immediately, the three of us jump out and get to work.

We dump a trash bag of spare clothes onto the ground, and Warren and I start stripping down and changing outfits, tossing everything we wore during the robbery back into the same bag.

Meanwhile, Chas reattaches the real license plate and burns the fake tag with a lighter, stomping the ashes into the dirt. Within just a couple of minutes, he takes off by himself, driving calmly and under the speed limit. Once he drops off the van at his aunt's house (to be handed over to its new owner), he'll return for us in his own car. Until then, we will just have to hang tight inside the warehouse.

Slipping through the hole we'd cut in the fence, Warren and I scour the building, room by room, checking to make sure that the place is empty.

Near the backside of the property, we stash the evidence bag among piles of trash, where no one would ever notice it.

Peeking my head through a broken window pane, I scan the alley behind the building. When I do this, a man cutting through the secluded backstreet spots me.

"What y'all doin' in there?" he shouts, staggering in our direction.

Right away, Warren and I start moving away from the windows, back in the direction we came.

Outside, the man is yelling to someone down the street about, "Some white boys fuckin' around in the buildin'." I can hear him rattling the fence, trying to find a way inside.

Forced to make a quick decision, we opt to bail while there's still an escape route. It's certainly not ideal for us to be outside wandering the streets in broad daylight, but we don't have much of a choice. We can't afford to get robbed while we've got the rare manuscripts in our backpacks or draw attention to ourselves with the police searching for us. So, we slip out the front while the men are still working on the fence in the back.

Across the street, Warren and I disappear into a vacant lot overgrown with waist-high grass, staying low to the ground until we reach a cluster of housing projects on the other side.

Surrounded by drab, plain brick buildings, we hurry down the block, smiling awkwardly at gawking residents. It doesn't help that our new outfits are extra preppy (a deliberate act we hoped would, in the event of our capture, dissuade law enforcement of our involvement in criminal activity). We look like two straight-laced white boys who got lost in the ghetto on their way to prep school.

As we walk past a group of guys hanging around a bass-thumping sedan, they instantly stop what they're doing and stare at us. One of them asks if we're lost, but I don't think he means it in a menacing way. He genuinely seems concerned for our safety. But we just keep moving and try not to make eye contact.

Behind one of the buildings, we find a spot that's mostly hidden. Facing a wooded area, we sit down in the grass with our backs up against a brick wall.

Now that we have a moment to spare, Warren calls Chas to set up a new extraction point. But after a long, drawn-out debate about where to meet, they finally decide to just pick up the conversation later, when Chas is nearby with the car.

"He's about to drop off the van," Warren says, while dialing another number. "Shouldn't be too much longer."

This time he puts the call on speakerphone so I can listen. I'm waiting for it to start ringing on the other end, but that never happens. Instead the line just clicks and Spencer starts rattling off everything he witnessed, as if he's just been sitting there, anxiously waiting for us to call.

"You guys burst out the door and some lady was chasing you!"

"Yes," Warren says.

"Then you peeled out in the van and almost hit her!"

"Yes, I know," Warren repeats.

"Holy shit, it was like something out of a movie!"

"Yes, I know. I was there!" Warren says. "I just need to know what happened after. Have the police shown up yet?"

Spencer says it took a while for anything to happen, much longer than he expected. Eventually the campus security showed up, but it was still a while before the police arrived.

"Now, they're everywhere," Spencer says. "It's turned into a big crime scene."

I can hear the anxiety in his voice. Having known Spencer for a while, I don't think he really wanted any of this to happen. The moment he told Warren about the manuscripts, it was all over, and there was no going back. He probably just assumed that Warren would inevitably abandon the outlandish plan, like so many times before. But that's clearly not what happened.

"I'll check back with you soon," Warren says. "Keep me posted if anything changes."

As we sit silently in the grass, frantic, disjointed snapshots of the robbery flash in my mind. The weight of what we've done is starting to sink in. Our lives will never be the same again. From now on, we will always be on the run, always looking over our shoulders.

Soon, Warren's phone starts ringing.

"Chas is getting close," he says. "Keep an eye out."

I rise to my feet, edge along the building, and peek around the corner. Across the vacant lot, directly in front of the drop spot, I see a police car creeping down the street. Then, as I turn back, at the opposite end of the block, I spot a second cruiser driving parallel to the other.

"Cops," I whisper to Warren. "I don't know if they saw me."

He's still on the phone with Chas, trying to navigate him to our location.

Dropping to my knees, I peek back around the corner of the building, bracing myself for the sight of multiple police cars headed straight for us.

"Be ready to run," I tell Warren. "Back through the woods."

I wait anxiously, but nothing happens. Peering around, I check to make sure that they're not coming at us from another direction. Just then, at the end of the block, I notice a gray Jeep turning onto our street.

"I think I see Chas," I tell Warren. "Ask him to flash his lights."

A moment later, the Jeep's headlights flicker on and off.

"Tell him to keep driving straight."

Tossing on our backpacks, we dart for the street, both of us frantically scanning the horizon for patrol cars.

As the two of us come into view, the Jeep accelerates in our direction, whipping a sharp U-turn in the middle of the street and screeching to a halt at the curb.

Way to be discreet, Chas, I think to myself, while jumping inside the car.

It's a short drive back to the house. Even though the windows are tinted, Warren and I recline low in the back seat, just to be safe. Lying there, face-to-face, neither one of us says a word, although I suppose we'll have plenty of time to talk about what we've done.

Chas reaches back and pats our legs, insisting that we are home free, but I don't think we'll ever truly be out of the woods.

When we get back to the house, everyone rushes off to handle their own affairs.

Warren immediately locks himself in the basement and starts dying his hair back to its original color. Luckily, only a handful of people saw him with blond hair: Betty, the employee who chased us, and a few eyewitnesses.

To avoid suspicion, I'll have to maintain my normal routine, which at the moment means completing my final exam for the semester. Thankfully it's the most meaningless one of all: tennis.

As I rush to class, cutting through the backstreets of campus, a steady cascade of snow begins to fall. One after another, the puffy snowflakes stick to my face until it's dripping wet, but my mind is elsewhere, concocting stories, rehearsing my performance—

What's that, officer? I beg your pardon. You say I was involved in . . . what? A book heist? At Transy? During finals week? You can't be serious! This must be a joke.

I'm so lost in thought that I slip on a patch of ice outside of the Rec Center, performing a panicked contortion while trying to regain my footing, much to the amusement of fellow students passing by.

After whisking down a few flights of stairs, I rush into the classroom and take a seat at the back just as the instructor is handing out tests. Sliding the paper onto my desk, he shoots me a scolding glare for nearly missing the exam and forcing him to actually flunk someone for an introduction to tennis class. However, a quick scan of the questions leaves me feeling less than confident. . . .

> If you hit the ball with enough backspin that it lands on your opponent's side of the court and then spins back over the net onto your side without your opponent touching it, whose point is it?

I'm sure on any other day it's a simple question with a simple answer, but today is not a typical day. I can't concentrate. My mind is racing. Any moment now the police could burst through the door looking for me.

According to USTA rules, what are the dimensions of a singles court?
A) 87 ft. x 32 ft.
B) 67 ft. x 23 ft.
C) 78 ft. x 27 ft.
D) 71 ft. x 22 ft.

What is the maximum diameter of the net cord or metal cable?
A) $2/3$ inch
B) $1/3$ inch
C) $1/4$ inch
D) $3/4$ inch

How tall is the net at the center?
A) 1 ft.
B) 2 ft.
C) 3 ft.
D) 4 ft.

What is the duration of the longest singles match in recorded history?
A) 4 hours, 10 minutes
B) 6 hours, 33 minutes
C) 9 hours, 48 minutes
D) 7 hours, 22 minutes

Eventually, I just start marking down answers at random. Most of the questions are multiple choice, so it's not very hard. There's no method to my decision-making, just whatever option stands out first. More than anything, I just need to get out of this classroom. It's my last exam for the semester, and I clearly have more important things to worry about than tennis trivia.

As I walk to the front of the classroom with my test in hand, there's no shortage of puzzled stares. I can see it on their faces—vaguely recognizable classmates whose names I never took the time to learn—they're trying to figure out how the guy who barely came to class could've possibly finished so quickly. Sadly, it's probably the only time in my life that I've been the first one to turn in a test.

When I slide the exam sheet on the instructor's desk, he glances up from his newspaper, startled. It takes him a moment to process what's happening. He hadn't expected anyone to be done so soon. I'm halfway out the door by the time he musters a faint, "Happy holidays!"

Back at the house, I pound on Warren's door using our secret knock, a one-three-one rhythm—*Knock . . . knock-knock-knock . . . knock*—but nothing happens. When I peek through the crack underneath the door, I notice that all the lights are turned out. Just when I start to think that he's actually not down there, I hear footsteps slowly creeping up the staircase, followed by the sound of the lock sliding open. By the time I get back up to my feet and open the door, he's already disappeared back down into the darkness, like some slithering cave creature.

Carefully descending the creaky staircase, I'm guided by faint flashes of white light coming from Warren's TV-VCR combo unit on the workbench. When I reach the bottom, I see him standing naked in front of the television, with his hair buzzed short.

"What happened to your hair?" I ask.

"Just in time," Warren says, with his eyes glued to the TV. "They're getting ready to talk about it."

I walk over to the bench and turn on the desk lamp, twisting the neck around so the beam shines on his face.

"It didn't look right with my hair long," Warren says, squinting and turning away from the light. "The color was all off."

I run my fingers over his short, prickly scalp hairs. "It's still got a bit of a sheen to it though, doesn't it?" I ask, while trying not to laugh.

"Trust me," Warren insists, "this is way better than before."

Just then the local news returns from commercials to a young reporter live at the scene of the crime.

"I'm standing outside of the Transylvania University library," she says, "where earlier today two men robbed and subdued a Special Collections librarian, before making off with some of the school's most prized possessions. Lexington Police are still combing over the crime scene, but at the moment they appear to have very little to go on, indicating that this may be the work of professionals."

Upon hearing this, Warren and I burst into laughter.

The reporter goes on to say that eyewitnesses described seeing a gray minivan flee from the scene, citing the make and model, along with our approximate age, height, and build. Before sending it back to the studio, she reads a tip-line phone number for viewers to call if they have any information regarding the crime.

Chas returns from his exam, and the two of us head out to retrieve the evidence bag from the warehouse. Meanwhile, Warren stays behind to fine-comb the basement for anything incriminating that we may have missed. Not to mention, considering the situation with his hair, everyone agrees that he should probably just lay low for a while.

At the warehouse, we park around the block, just in case we're walking into some kind of ambush. After slipping through the fence hole, we creep inside the building, peeking around corners and sending each other hand signals like we're commandos on a top-secret mission. In the faint evening light, the heaps of trash look like curled-up bodies. Tiptoeing around the dark mounds, I find myself staring distrustfully at the shadows, seeing human qualities in bags of garbage.

In the back, buried among the many piles of debris, I dig out the plastic bag exactly where I left it. Wasting no time, I sling it over my shoulder while Chas leads the way back out of the building the same way that we came, treading cautiously down dark and broken sidewalks.

The rest of the night we disperse the contents of the bag among different dumpsters throughout the city. Chas drives while I spot the containers. There's nothing too scientific about it—some clothes here, a few zip ties there—the only criteria being that the bins are far apart from one another and not in view of security cameras. Everything is handled with leather gloves, which are themselves the last items to be tossed.

———

Spencer is smoking a joint in the living room, staring off into space. He jolts when we burst through the door, clearly startled, though he tries to play it off like nothing happened.

"Warren's gone," he says, sinking back into the couch and coolly tapping the joint onto an ash tray, as if he hasn't been sitting here in a deep state of paranoia obsessing over all the shady things that Warren could be doing.

I start pounding on Warren's door, but Spencer quickly stops me.

"Already tried that," he says. "Trust me, he's not down there."

Obviously we can't call him because he doesn't own a cell phone, and seeing how I just trashed his burner phone, that's no longer an option.

Just as I sit down, Warren calmly strolls through the front door, wearing a baseball cap over his newly auburn-colored buzzed hair, and lugging a backpack over his shoulder.

"Hey guys," he says, while casually walking through the living room and searching his pockets for keys.

"Where have you been?" I ask.

"Just had to take care of a few last-minute things," he responds, unlocking his bedroom door and disappearing into the basement.

We all stare at each other, confused and racking our brains for a reason to give Warren the benefit of the doubt. Then, without speaking, as if on cue, we all get up and follow him downstairs.

"What kind of last-minute things?" I ask, before even reaching the bottom of the staircase.

Flinging his muddy Wallabees onto the floor, Warren awkwardly spins around, surprised to find us all standing there. Although that doesn't stop him from stripping off all of his clothes directly in front of us.

"Actually," he blurts out, while stumbling around with his jeans pulled down to his ankles, "I'm glad everyone's here. We need to talk."

Once he's done changing into his Adidas track suit, Warren joins the rest of us seated around the coffee table.

"So," he sighs, searching for the right place to begin. "I was at the library—*the UK library,*" he instantly clarifies. "I had to send out some last-minute emails before it closed for winter break."

"What kind of emails?" I ask.

"To our friend in Amsterdam . . . and others," he mutters.

"What others?"

"Well, you know, there's been a lot going on," he dithers. "I didn't want to worry you guys. I mean, everything is fine. It's no big deal. It's just, our guy in Amsterdam is getting a little impatient, that's all. I had to break the news to him that *Birds of America* is no longer for sale. He wasn't happy about that. Now he's starting to question everything I say. He thinks we're fucking with him. And if we can't provide some kind of documentation proving that we have the other items, I think he's going to walk away."

As the news sinks in, a wave of disappointment engulfs the room, followed by a collective "Fuck."

"Which is why I set up an appointment to get the books appraised," Warren says, dropping a bombshell.

"What?" We all erupt at once.

"I had to make an executive decision!" he pleads.

Completely stunned, we stare at each other in silence, trying to make sense of it all.

"Also," Warren adds, grimacing, "the appointment is in three days . . . in New York City."

The hits just keep on coming.

I hadn't imagined things playing out this way. The plan was to stash the books away for a while, and then, when the time was right, we would transport them to Europe.

Backtracking, Warren says that he can always cancel the appointment, but he's worried that we might lose our contact in Amsterdam, in which case finding another buyer may not be so easy. The more he explains himself, the more I see where he's coming from. Still, with Warren, there's no way of ever really knowing the truth. The real story always lies somewhere within a myriad of possibilities. Eventually you find yourself just going along with him because you have no other choice.

The four of us hang out in the basement late into the night, drinking bourbon and recounting the day's dreadful events. It's obvious that no one wants to be alone right now, like some sort of coping mechanism, a way of dealing with what we've done.

Lying on the cold floor, I stare up at the nail-covered joists, listening to my roommates' creaky footsteps on the wooden floorboards above. They have no idea what's going on down here, right under their feet, as if we're living side-by-side in parallel worlds.

After a while, the guys start to wonder if I'm all right.

"He hasn't said anything in like an hour," Chas mutters under his breath.

I pretend not to hear them over the Beastie Boys blaring from the stereo—

> *Got weight on my shoulders and things on my mind*
> *The sky is falling and I'm falling behind*

However, one distinct noise consistently rises above the rest, like the gut-wrenching sound of a car crash echoing in my head, as if it just happened moments ago.

When Betty screamed, I felt my path suddenly change course, like a train switching tracks, crossing over into a new world, with no way of going back.

Much of my recollection is hazy, but one fading, dreamlike memory remains—an out-of-body vision of myself standing frozen inside the museum during the robbery, with a glassy portal floating in front of me like an upright puddle of water. All of a sudden it occurred to me that I'd been searching for it my entire life, always hurtling toward it—whatever *it* is— to this moment, right here, right now.

7

NEW AMSTERDAM

A couple days later, the four of us pile into my car for the long drive north, telling our families that we're going on a ski trip in West Virginia, and we'll be back before Christmas.

Early on, the trip takes an unexpected turn when Warren informs us that his trusted appraiser in New York is none other than the multibillion-dollar British auction giant, Christie's.

"They're very discreet," Warren assures us, explaining that our business is with the private sales department, and not the public auction house. "It's all confidential."

Coasting down the highway, I take my foot off the pedal, unsure of what to do. *Should I pull over? Turn the car around?* We were supposed to keep this secret close to the chest. Instead, we're practically walking straight up to the world's most prominent art dealer with a suitcase full of stolen works. For all we know, Christie's could've already alerted the authorities. We could be walking into a trap.

Warren says that we should act before word of the robbery spreads outside of Kentucky, at which point everyone will be on the lookout for the books.

"If we are ever going to do this, the time is now," he says. "They don't know anything about me. All they have is a fake email address."

This is just the kind of stunt that Warren would pull, yet somehow I never see them coming. Of course, he already knows that we will go along with his plan, seeing how we've been driving for hours now. The least we can do is scope out the scene.

We stop for the night at a cheap motel off the interstate near Harrisburg, opting to finish the last leg of the trip in the morning. Warren's revelation seems to have put a damper on group morale.

It's cold and rainy outside, so we just have pizzas delivered to the room. There's not much to see around here anyway. Besides, it's probably best that we keep a low profile.

As we huddle around the television, I realize that this is the new life I have to look forward to—lying low in shitty motel rooms, eating greasy delivery food while watching re-runs of *Seinfeld,* always paying with cash, always watching my back, always covering my tracks as if I don't even exist.

I guess it could be worse.

———

Sometime around noon we exit the Holland Tunnel to gridlocked Manhattan traffic, looping around St. John's Park, and inching our way uptown through the tree-lined streets of Greenwich Village. After a while, the historic red-brick townhouses turn into boxy, billboard-clad mid-rises, while the sleek skyscrapers looming in the distance grow nearer and taller.

Before I know it, I'm driving straight through the center of Times Square, gawking up at the patchwork of brightly-lit screens advertising everything imaginable, from Broadway shows to multinational banks.

The sidewalks are jam-packed with tourists, forcing me to slam on my brakes on more than once as someone suddenly darts into the street for no apparent reason.

Meanwhile, taxis are honking at me from every direction, but I can't figure out why. *It must be my Kentucky license plate,* I think.

Amid the babel, unbeknownst to everyone else, I'm buzzing inside with excitement. Ever since I was a kid, I've been completely obsessed with New York City.

I was born upstate in Poughkeepsie, which is about an hour-and-a-half train ride north along the Hudson. My dad, a mechanical engineer for IBM, was routinely transferred from one location to another. He and my mother first moved to Colorado (where my brother was born), then back to Poughkeepsie (where I was born), then back to Colorado again, then to North Carolina (where my sister was born), before finally settling in Kentucky.

Still, every year, no matter where we were living, the whole family would pile into our station wagon for the long cross-country trip back to upstate New York. Every single time, I would beg my parents to take me into the city, but they always refused. Sometimes we were so close that I could actually see the Manhattan skyscrapers shimmering in the distance.

"Why would you want to go there?" they'd ask, disgusted at the very idea of it. "The city is dirty and dangerous and expensive. You don't want to go there—trust us!"

It didn't help that my grandparents backed them up, recounting stories of being mugged in broad daylight or returning to find their cars tireless and resting on cinder blocks. In time, I came to believe that whenever you drove into the city, your tires would be stolen, that was just part of the deal.

Both sides of my family came from long lines of poor, working-class European immigrants who moved to New York City long ago. They had spent generations trying to get out of the city, so naturally the thought of going back was inconceivable.

After a while, my obsession with the city became somewhat of a sensitive subject, like the black sheep of the family, whose name we do not speak—*The city? Oh, gawd no! We don't tawk about the city.* Just the phrase, "the city," came to represent something I was supposed to fear, but that didn't keep me from dreaming about it.

To me, the city was a magical place where anything was possible. *The city that never sleeps*—I just loved the sound of that, as if it were a living, breathing entity all its own. You could find anything you wanted, at any hour of the day. The city was the beatnik free-spiritedness I discovered in Kerouac's spontaneous prose and in the untamed adolescent exploits on screen in *The Basketball Diaries*. The truth is, the city was anything you wanted it to be—an endless world of possibilities.

Then one year, after being denied my request to visit Manhattan yet again, I retreated to a corner of my uncle's house in upstate New York to sulk. From the other room, I could overhear my parents explaining the story.

"What, the kid wants to go to the city?" my uncle demanded in his thick New York accent, shocked that it was the first time he'd heard about it. "Yeah, sure, I'll take 'em," he said, without even being asked to do so. "I gotta run down there in the morning anyway—some business I gotta take care of."

I was never really sure what he did for a living—*some kind of accountant, maybe?* I just knew that he was a towering, smooth-talking salesman who seemed to have *a guy* for everything.

"You in the market for a hot tub, my man?" he'd ask.

"No, Uncle Tony, I'm a child."

"Well, just sayin' . . . *I know a guy*. He'll give you a helluva deal. Just somethin' for you to think about."

In reality, Tony was a big teddy bear who would do just about anything for his family. If I needed a kidney, he would be the first one in line to donate.

"What?" he'd say, brushing it off. "I wasn't using mine anyway—fuhgeddaboudit!"

When Tony heard that year after year I'd been begging my parents to take me into the city, he didn't hesitate to offer. *No big deal,* he would say. I doubt he even had business there. He probably just said that so my parents would accept his offer—and surprisingly, it worked. Just like that, thanks to an offhand, adult comment, my many years of torment finally came to an end, teaching me a valuable life lesson in the futility of adolescent dreams.

Joined by my brother and two cousins, we headed out the following morning, driving south from Schenectady in my uncle's old Cadillac for a boys' day out in the city.

I slept for the first couple of hours with my head wedged in a vibrating crevice between the window and back seat, waking periodically to kidney shots from my cousins wrestling in the seat next to me, as well as the occasional roadside pit stop.

At Taco Bell, my cousin dared his little brother to eat an entire packet of hot sauce—a challenge he promptly accepted and then vomited all over himself.

After a quick wardrobe change, we were back on the road with only about an hour to go.

My cousins insisted on playing the same song over and over on the car stereo, from a new CD one of them bought by an oddly named band called Chumbawamba. The first time around, the song was tolerable enough, but after twenty minutes of it, I was beyond ready for the drive to be over—and to my surprise, it nearly was.

> *I get knocked down, but I get up again*
> *You are never gonna keep me down*
> *I get knocked down, but I get up again*
> *You are never gonna keep me down*
> *I get knocked down, but I get up again*
> *You are never gonna keep me down*
> *I get knocked down, but I get up again*

We were somewhere near Hackensack when smoke started pouring out from underneath the hood, and Uncle Tony pulled the car over to the side of the road.

From the back seat, I watched anxiously as he propped open the hood and fanned away the billowing smoke, while the car rocked back and forth from the swarms of vehicles on the interstate passing by, uncomfortably close.

The engine probably just overheated, I told myself, trying to remain optimistic. *That's a thing, right?*

But as ten minutes turned into twenty, and then twenty into thirty, I started to get concerned. Whenever we tried to find out what was happening, Uncle Tony would tell us to get back inside the car. Finally, when I heard him calling a tow truck on his cell phone, I knew that I'd have to accept the sad truth—we would not be going to the city.

Eventually, when the truck arrived, I could tell that Tony was pissed about how much it was going to cost him, which made me feel even worse, seeing how the trip was entirely for me.

"Never had a single problem before this," he grumbled, trying to schmooze the driver, while loud, mechanized chains pulled the car onto the flatbed. "Just tryin' to take my boys out for a nice day in the city!"

Since Tony snatched up the only passenger seat in the cabin, the rest of us had no choice but to ride inside the broken-down Cadillac on top of the tow truck.

Climbing up onto the flatbed, I settled into the hot, sticky, leather driver's seat for the long air conditioning-less drive back upstate.

As the truck rumbled to a start, I peered out over the steering wheel at the Manhattan skyline glistening on the horizon. Little did I know, it would be many more years before I finally made it there, as a nineteen-year-old with a group of friends transporting stolen artwork.

—

We book a room at the Midtown Hilton, the same hotel that Warren and Spencer stayed at a year ago when they met with the mysterious man in Central Park. It's hard to believe that we're all here, a year later, in the same spot, with the stolen books (most of them, anyway).

Since Christie's is only a few blocks away, our first order of business is to execute a dry run, just to make sure we're all prepared for our meeting in the morning.

We make our way toward Rockefeller Center, fighting fierce holiday crowds and bone-chilling winds whipping between the high-rises of Midtown. Shivering uncontrollably, the four of us rush down 6th Avenue, twisting and shrieking past Radio City Music Hall in search of warmth.

At a sidewalk stand selling winter accessories, we cover our bodies with hats, gloves, and scarves, desperately throwing our money at the vendor without even asking for prices. The old man laughs and hands us our change before moving on to the next shivering out-of-towner.

Soon, the sleek department stores of Rockefeller Center morph into a stately limestone structure with tall multistoried windows displaying a variety of artwork inside. Above the glass canopy of the entryway soar three separate flags: The Stars and Stripes, The Union Jack, and the solid-red banner of Christie's.

On the other side of the gold-plated revolving door, we find a sterile, polished lobby branching off into public galleries crowded with tourists. Immediately, the four of us split up.

As I'm scoping the place out, it occurs to me that we may be in over our heads. There are cameras and security personnel everywhere. *Of all the places to get an appraisal, why would Warren choose one of the most renowned and well-guarded auction houses in the world?* Then I recall that he subscribes to a particular philosophy which holds that if you're going to break the law, you should do it in plain sight, because no one would expect that. Like when he used to smoke joints directly underneath the school security camera. *Just act normal,* he would say. *If anyone sees us, they'll just presume we're smoking cigarettes.* By conditioning himself to believe his own lies, Warren had mastered the art of deception. But just because you've gotten away with something for a while doesn't necessarily mean that it's foolproof. Eventually someone is bound to smell the smoke and start looking for the fire.

After wandering around 30 Rock for a while, we eventually hail a town car across the street from St. Patrick's Cathedral.

Maneuvering into traffic, the driver—a balding, fast-talking New Yorker—asks us where we're headed.

Without thinking, I just blurt out, "Ground Zero."

The guys nod their heads in agreement, as if it just goes without saying that we should pay our respects before anything else. It's hard to believe that it has already been three years since the attack.

Eying us in the rearview mirror, the driver tries to make conversation by asking us the typical questions like "Where are you from?" and "What brings you to the city?"

We respond with off-the-cuff lies, until Warren tactlessly rolls up the divider window, muttering something about needing to talk with his coworkers about business-related matters in private.

Once we're alone, he pulls out a bottle of bourbon from his messenger bag and starts passing it around. Chas cranks up the volume on the radio and soon we're all laughing and rapping along to Biggie Smalls while taking swigs of the hometown brew. Every now and then, in short spurts, we are somehow able to put the other stuff out of our minds—the guilt of what we've done, how our lives will never be the same, and the mere fact that we are being hunted by the police at this very moment.

When we step out of the taxi in lower Manhattan, crowds of onlookers are lining the sidewalk, pressed up against tall, immovable, steel-wire barricades cordoning off a square plot of empty land for multiple blocks. We find an opening along the fence and stare down into the pit like somber spectators at a sporting event. Down below, rumbling dump trucks move in and out of the crater via makeshift off-ramps.

There are layers upon layers of activity taking place, but from up here it just looks like they're pushing around dirt. After all this time, it's hard to believe that more progress has not been made. By seeing the sight in person, you start to get a sense of the scale of destruction caused that day. September 11th, 2001, is one of those rare dates when everyone of a certain age remembers exactly where they were and what they were doing when they first learned of the attack.

I for one remember the scene like it was yesterday. It was my junior year of high school, and I had accidentally left behind my graphing calculator in chemistry class (one of those hefty devices they make students buy every year and subsequently guard with their lives because they're so expensive). So I rushed through the bustling, locker-lined hallways, dodging fellow students—including Warren, who in typical fashion tried to knock my books out of my hand because he could tell I was running late—while trying to retrieve my calculator before the next class started.

When I arrived, the classroom was empty, except for my teacher who was staring up at the television mounted on the wall. I apologized for interrupting, but she promptly shushed me. I didn't think much about it at the time. *Maybe she's busy preparing a video for the next class or something—who knows?* I was just focused on getting in and out of there as quickly as possible. I went straight for my desk and found the calculator exactly where I'd left it, in the book rack underneath the seat, as usual. Turning back toward the door, I apologized a second time for the intrusion—but she shushed me again. This time I took notice, because her behavior was so out of character.

Peering up at the TV, I finally saw that she was watching live news coverage of a terrible disaster in New York City, which stopped me dead in my tracks. Aerial images showed one of the Twin Towers on fire, clouds of black smoke pouring into the bright morning sky. Witnesses on the ground reported seeing a plane fly into the building, but it hadn't been confirmed yet. For the longest time, my teacher and I just stood there, speechless, staring up at the television screen in disbelief.

By the time I got to my next class, everyone was talking about the incident, but no one seemed to have any answers. Classes were cancelled for the day, and the entire school was corralled into the gymnasium. There were rumors that a second plane had crashed into the other World Trade Center building, and before long, we heard that a third plane had hit the Pentagon. At that point, it was clear that we were under attack.

Then the unthinkable happened. Huddled around a TV in the cafeteria, we watched in horror as the one hundred-plus floors of the South Tower collapsed to the ground like a house of cards, sending monstrous plumes of thick, gray debris down the corridors of lower Manhattan, engulfing hordes of bystanders in the streets.

All around me, students and faculty alike gasped in shock. Some held each other and wept. But every time we thought we'd seen the worst of it, another horrible headline would flash across the screen. The latest reports were that a fourth hijacked plane had crashed in rural Pennsylvania. For the first time, US airspace was completely shut down and all domestic flights grounded. There was no way of knowing when, where, or for that matter *if,* there would be another attack. Even in central Kentucky, far away from the tragedies and not exactly a prime target for terrorists, we were genuinely concerned for our safety.

In the end, when the unthinkable happened yet again and the North Tower collapsed, just like the other one had, leaving behind a scene of devastation that would take years to recover from, that's when everyone exited the school building en masse, unsure of what the future held.

———

After visiting Ground Zero, we grab a drink at an old Irish pub on Beekman Street that's been around since the Depression era. Squeezing into a sticky booth in the corner, the four of us start knocking back glasses of bourbon while strategizing about our appointment in the morning.

Seeing how we don't really know what we're walking into, we decide to split into two groups. Since Warren is the one who's been in contact with Christie's, and Spencer has the most knowledge of the manuscripts' provenance, the two of them will attend the meeting, while Chas and I remain outside with the books. Assuming they're not immediately arrested in an undercover sting operation, Spencer will call to inform us that everything is in order, at which point we'll hand over the books in the Christie's lobby. After that, who knows what will happen?

It's not long before Chas is slurring his speech and lecturing Warren and Spencer about how to handle themselves in the meeting. He regurgitates lines from business books he's read, uttering phrases like, "Try not to appear desperate," and, "You've got the leverage. Let them know you're willing to walk away."

I have to remind him that we are not here to sell the books—we're just getting them appraised.

Chas insists that he understands, but a moment later he's off on another tangent, fantasizing about all the things he could do with the money.

"You know," he says, airily, "many economists have predicted a depression within the next decade. Just imagine if we could ride into the crash with that kind of untaxed cash—that's how empires are built!"

Of course whenever Chas says "we," the three of us know that he's really just talking about himself. He still has no clue that we're in this for something else, for something greater than money, which is something he could never understand. What that thing is exactly, we haven't quite figured out yet—but whatever it is,

I have no doubt that it's the complete opposite of Chas's motivation.

Before I know it, I find myself hiding out in the bathroom, unable to listen to Chas's voice any longer. Staring at my reflection in the mirror, I barely even recognize myself anymore. I feel like a stranger in my own world. *How did it come to this?* I wonder. *What am I doing here?* I should be at home celebrating the holidays with my family, not here listening to Chas talk about how he's going to build a dynasty. Or was it an empire?

As I'm leaving the men's room, something comes over me. I can't go back to the table—*I just can't do it.* Chas's presence is chipping away at my soul. Impulsively, I sneak out the opposite end of the pub without the others seeing me.

Speed-walking down the street, I quickly turn the corner at the end of the block. Before I know it, I'm rushing through a tree-lined park like an escaped mental patient, briefly skirting the palatial exterior of City Hall. *What am I doing?* I ask myself, while looking around to see if I'm being followed. *Maybe I've just had too much to drink. Am I being irrational? But what's right or wrong anymore? Just a few days ago, I robbed a museum and helped tie up an old woman in the process.*

Eventually they're going to start calling and looking for me. Luckily, my cell phone is already dead, so at least I have that as an excuse. But moving forward, I don't really have a plan. I just had to get out of there and away from Chas as quickly as possible, like an itch desperately needing to be scratched. The moment I stepped outside, the agony instantly melted away.

Maybe, at least for a little while, I can try to forget about everything else and just appreciate my time here in the city I've always dreamed about visiting. The truth is, this is probably the closest to normal my life will ever be again.

With no particular destination in mind, I continue heading uptown, crisscrossing through the sett stone side streets of Soho, admiring the rows of cast-iron façades dotted with art galleries and designer boutiques.

Finally, when I spot the violet flags of NYU draped from brown-brick buildings—the first recognizable landmark in a while—I start scouring the lively campus blocks for Washington Square Park.

With the sun nearly set, I sit down on a bench overlooking the famous arch, towering above a giant, twinkling Christmas tree. Glancing around the dusk-stained park, I try to envision the countless spectacles that have unfolded here over the years, from Ginsberg reading *Howl* before packed crowds and musicians like Dylan and Buddy Holly busking for fortunate passersby to endless sunny Sundays of dancing hippies on roller skates and chess players locked in silent battles in the shady, tree-covered corner.

Once I'm done daydreaming in the park, I swing through the Village for a drink. Through an unmarked door on Bedford, I find a former speakeasy and favorite watering hole among distinguished writers. The cozy pub's walls are lined with authors' photographs alongside their books, from Faulkner to Steinbeck to F. Scott Fitzgerald. Near the crackling fireplace, I people-watch and sip on White Russians while jotting down thoughts in a notepad. My most recent masterpiece: "Caucasians & dead writers on the wall." I know it doesn't sound like much, but by the end of the night the cryptic lines will form full verses.

Leaning over the bar, a young, baby-faced uniformed soldier asks me to take a picture of him with his parents, and I gratefully oblige. As I focus the camera, determined not to fuck up this important moment with my drunkenness, they shoot each other concerned looks, puzzled as to why it's taking me so long.

"Cheese," I finally mutter, hesitantly, giving them the signal.

They hug each other tightly, while Mom and Dad do their best to fight back tears.

To show their appreciation, they insist on buying me a drink. I politely decline, but they won't have it, so we order a round and raise our glasses to the holidays. I learn that they live just around the corner, and that the young man, who decided to join the Army after 9/11, is returning home from his first tour of duty in Afghanistan. They haven't seen each other in more than a year.

Before long, they start asking me questions about myself—the usual, like "Where are you from?" and "What do you do for a living?"

For some reason, I tell them that my name is Walter Beckman, an art dealer from Boston. I don't know why I say this; it just slips out.

Drunk and flustered, I excuse myself to use the restroom and hastily sneak out the exit (my signature move, apparently), regretful that I never thanked the young man for his service.

Continuing uptown, I stagger through dense, snow-dusted city blocks of pizza shops, laundromats, and delis, while stopping at all sorts of bars along the way for just long enough to finish a drink and jot down some more thoughts in my notepad.

Leaving a dive bar in Hell's Kitchen, it suddenly occurs to me that I have no idea where the hotel is located, other than it's in Midtown somewhere between Rockefeller Center and Central Park. Whenever I ask people on the street for directions, they lower their gazes and barrel past me. Although, I realize I look like a deranged drunkard, and I can't really blame them. Occasionally someone is kind enough to point, and like a sad, lost animal, I scamper off in that direction.

Eventually, when I pass the Lincoln Center, I realize that I've gone too far, but at least now I know where I am. Turning down 65th Street, it's not long before I spot the wooded enclave of Central Park.

I follow a quiet walking path, passing under an old stone bridge, then another, meandering in the direction that I think will put me somewhere near the lower east side of the park.

At a rocky hillside, I climb up and lie down for a while on a powdery outcropping, next to an odd, wooden lean-to, with the illuminated high-rises of Midtown looming in the background. Gazing up at the wintry night sky, I feel fluttering snowflakes settling on my face and dissolving into tiny puddles. As I start to doze off, I can't help but marvel at how peaceful it is out here. For a moment, you can almost forget that you're still in the heart of the city.

———

In the morning, I let myself into the hotel room, hungover and reeking of booze. The guys are getting ready for the meeting, and immediately they start going off on me. Apparently they were worried I'd been arrested.

Now that the alcohol has worn off, I feel somewhat bad about ditching them. While getting dressed, I do a sort of half-apology, pretending that I just had too much to drink and wandered off, only for my phone to die later on, before passing out in Central Park.

Though visibly annoyed, they seem to get over it pretty quickly, apparently just relieved that I wasn't arrested and managed to turn up in time for the meeting.

Before leaving, we carefully arrange the books inside a rolling suitcase while going over the plan one last time, though it's clear that there's a lot we can't prepare for. Once Warren and Spencer are inside Christie's, there's no telling what will happen. For all we know, the Feds could already be onto us.

Strutting down busy 6th Avenue, we receive our fair share of curious looks. Dressed in black overcoats, suits, leather gloves, and sunglasses, we look like baby-faced mobsters in training. Not to mention, the lone, black, hardshell suitcase rolling at my side only seems to add to the mystique.

Turning the corner at 50th Street, underneath the vintage marquee of Radio City Music Hall, we walk to the end of the block and make our way into Rockefeller Center. At the opposite end of the plaza, Chas and I break off, taking a seat on a bench overlooking the ice rink, while Warren and Spencer continue on to Christie's. Moments later, I watch as they're greeted by a doorman before disappearing inside the building.

The two of us sit in silence while scanning the crowd, surrounded on all sides by towering art deco high-rises loaded with surveillance devices. Considering Rockefeller Center is one of the most secure sites in Manhattan—and for that matter, the entire country—it's safe to assume that many of those cameras are currently trained on us.

Meanwhile, scores of sightseers shuffle around us, vying for views of the famous Rockefeller Center Christmas tree, with the statue of Prometheus in the foreground, stealing fire from the gods for humanity. Behind the gilded cast bronze sculpture, carved into a red, granite wall, an inscription reads: *Prometheus, teacher in every art, brought the fire that hath proved to mortals a means to mighty ends.*

Whenever the tourists catch sight of us, alarmed expressions spread over their faces. Their eyes immediately focus on the closely guarded suitcase wedged between us, which I haven't let go of since we got here.

It's only been a few years since the September 11th attacks, and these days it seems like everyone is on edge, especially in New York City. You see the slogan plastered everywhere, from billboards to subway cars: *If you see something, say something.*

At first I think it's just in my head, but the longer we sit there in silence, frantically monitoring our surroundings, the more attention we seem to attract. After a long and awkward interval, I'm beginning to worry that we might actually have an issue on our hands. Just then, my cell phone starts to ring.

"We're good," Spencer says, in his usual, deadpan tone.

He's never really been much of a talker, so I have to squeeze him for more information, in case he's already been nabbed and turned by the authorities. For all I know, this could be a setup, although I'm probably just overreacting.

"So, *everything* is good?" I ask.

"Yeah, it's all good."

"Is it though?"

"Yeah," he says. *"It is."*

"Dixie's not dead?"

"Not that I know of," he says, starting to lose his patience.

"What's that supposed to mean?"

"I'll meet you at the entrance," Spencer says.

Nearby, anxious bystanders are eavesdropping on my conversation, trying to figure out what kind of shady business we're up to. It doesn't help that, after ending the phone call, I turn to Chas and say, "It's time," at which point we both calmly stand up and walk away, with the mysterious suitcase in tow. It's just the sort of thing a criminal would say in a gangster flick, right before walking into a dicey situation.

From the bench, it's only a short walk over to Christie's, where a smiling attendant is holding the door open for me while Chas lingers behind to keep watch.

Just inside the lobby, I find Spencer—unmistakable in his dapper vintage suit—nervously waiting for me. With the doorman hovering nearby, I try not to say much out loud. As I hand Spencer the suitcase, I stare into his eyes, hoping to glean some sort of indication as to how the meeting is going. But, as usual, he gives me nothing—he just turns and walks away.

The attendant, clearly surprised by our shady hand-off, scurries ahead of me to open the door, all the while politely smiling as if it were just business as usual.

Outside, Chas and I try to blend in with the crowd and appear a little less conspicuous than before. We stroll around Rockefeller Plaza, exploring NBC Studios and the adjoining tourist shops, while keeping our eyes peeled for Warren and Spencer.

A little while later, as I'm perusing *Seinfeld* merchandise, we spot the two of them leaving Christie's with the suitcase. Walking in the opposite direction, they're seemingly so engrossed in conversation that they forget to call us, as we discussed.

When we catch up with them down the block, standing in front of the Simon & Schuster building, they both immediately quiet down, their lively exchange diminished to awkward half-smiles.

Assuming they're just trying to be discreet, I suggest that we walk to Central Park, where they can fill us in on the details.

Along the way, I'm dying for some information, even just a morsel. Unable to contain myself, I start murmuring questions under my breath. "Good or bad?" I ask. "Thumbs up or thumbs down?"

Warren and Spencer stare questioningly at one another, unsure of where to start.

Before they can respond, I stop them. "No, no, no," I balk. "It's okay. We can wait."

Warren leads us to a bench overlooking a partially frozen pond, just across the street from The Plaza Hotel, and says that it's the exact same spot where he met "The Man in the Green Scarf" over a year ago. He starts to retell the story, but I quickly cut him off—

"Could you just tell us about Christie's?"

After a moment of reflection, Warren starts from the beginning, explaining that, Mr. Leckey, the rare book specialist we were scheduled to meet with, couldn't make the appointment, so his associate, an employee named Melanie, filled in. She escorted Warren and Spencer to a conference room, where they introduced themselves as Mr. Williams and Mr. Stephens, respectively. They claimed to be the sole representatives of Walter Beckman, a private collector from Boston, who recently inherited several rare manuscripts he wanted to have appraised. When Melanie asked to examine the books, Spencer called my cell phone. Moments later, we made the handoff in the lobby. When Spencer returned with the suitcase, she conducted an inspection of the manuscripts, while taking detailed notes for the appraisal. According to Warren, she was "blown away" by the rareness and exquisite condition of the pieces and apparently "not suspicious whatsoever." However, I find that hard to believe, seeing how everyone, from the mysterious man in Central Park to the Amsterdam dealer has been put off by our young age. Still, Melanie said that she would pass along the information to Mr. Leckey, and someone would be in touch within the coming weeks.

For some reason, when Warren finishes retelling the story, the conclusion feels anticlimactic. Although I'm not really sure what I expected. After all, it was just a preliminary appraisal meeting. I guess, in the back of my mind, I was worried that the Christie's representatives would instantly see right through our charade. After all, a simple internet search would reveal the details of the robbery. Our one saving grace is that Christie's only has security-camera footage of us, with no way of divulging our true identities.

As swells of sunlight break through the clouds, cascading over the snow-covered meadow, the four of us take one last stroll around the park before we have to head back home to Kentucky.

Savoring my final moments in the city, I climb up a boulder overlooking the pond, stepping cautiously in my dress shoes on the slippery surface. Just days before Christmas, packs of sightseers are roaming about, reveling in the holiday spirit. There's something almost magical about Manhattan this time of year, a feeling both palpable and contagious.

Peering down at the walking path, I see Warren and Spencer standing off to the side, speaking quietly to one another. They've been acting kind of strange ever since they left the meeting, although it's probably just lingering nerves. These tense situations tend to stay with you for a while, replaying over and over in your mind as you analyze every little detail.

On the way back to the hotel, Chas and I start asking follow-up questions as the details of the meeting begin to set in.

So, you really think it went well?

And you don't think they were suspicious at all?

How long did they say it'll take to hear back from them?

Finally, Chas asks the one question we should've asked from the very beginning: "How are they going to contact you?"

Before this, I hadn't really thought about it. I just presumed they would remain in contact through whichever fake email address Warren used to set up the meeting in the first place.

Warren and Spencer glance at each other out the corner of their eyes. A long silence follows as we wait for one of them to respond.

Finally, Spencer speaks up. "I gave them my cell phone number," he says.

"What do you mean you gave them your cell phone number?" Chas asks.

"At the end of the meeting, they asked for a contact number," Spencer continues. "I just sort of blurted it out."

"You mean you gave them your *real* phone number?" I ask.

"As in the one that can be traced back to you?" Chas adds.

"Yes," Spencer says, flustered. "That one."

"What the fuck were you thinking?" Chas erupts, in the middle of a busy Midtown sidewalk, forcing startled pedestrians to guardedly sidestep around us.

"I don't know," Spencer groans, trying to defend himself. "They'd already seen me talking on my phone when I called you. I don't know what I was thinking. It all happened so quickly. By the time I realized what I'd done, it was too late. . . I think we might be okay though."

"Oh, you *think we might be okay*?" Chas mocks him. "Great—that's just fucking great!"

Meanwhile, Warren is staring quietly at the ground, grimacing, still reeling from the blow.

"Come on," I say to everyone. "Let's talk about this inside."

Back in the hotel room, the four of us bitterly pack our bags while arguing with one another. Even though it's a big deal—*a really big deal*—I try to downplay the gravity of the situation to take some pressure off of Spencer. The truth is, he's never really been cut out for this line of work. He wouldn't even be here if it weren't for Warren. Then again, none of us would.

The argument continues all the way down to the lobby while we're waiting for the car to arrive. When the valet pulls up, he hands me the keys and awkwardly watches us hurl our bags into the trunk, bickering back and forth the entire time. I'm so distracted that I peel out of the parking garage without tipping—or even acknowledging—the driver.

As I'm navigating through Midtown traffic, inching toward the Lincoln Tunnel, Chas demands that I turn the car around and head back to Christie's.

"We'll give them an email address or something," he pleads. "We just have to make them delete the phone number—that's all there is to it."

"And you don't think that would look even more suspicious?" Spencer asks.

"I don't care if it looks suspicious, Spencer! It's better than going to prison!" Chas snaps, turning to the rest of us for support. "We have to at least try, right?"

I glance at Warren in the passenger seat, and in that moment there's an unspoken awareness between us: We are not going back to Christie's. Chas is the only one who's actually angry about the situation—*furious*, even. For some reason, the rest of us are oddly content with the outcome, as if it were meant to be.

"I don't think it's going to happen," Warren says, breaking the news to Chas.

"Are you guys fucking kidding me?" he shouts, punching the back of the headrest, demanding that I either turn the car around or let him out.

But I ignore Chas's ultimatum and just keep driving. When we reach New Jersey, on the other side of the Hudson, he finally gives up.

Once again, we take turns driving throughout the night, except for Chas, who refuses to speak to us (although I can't say that I'm too disappointed about that). The ride back home is even more uncomfortable than it was on the way up, when Warren first informed us that his trusted appraiser was Christie's—however, our latest predicament concerns a different set of circumstances altogether. With the radio signal fading in and out, the somber mood inside the car is only worsened by intermittent segments of breaking news that the NSA has been spying on millions of Americans without warrants, stoking our worst dystopian fears of government surveillance.

After my shift at the wheel, I move to the backseat and eventually fall asleep with my face pressed up against the cold window, waking occasionally to blurred glimpses of black, frozen mountains and sweeping tracts of illuminated oil-refineries like futuristic hellscapes. Adrift somewhere between dream and reality, I envision myself lying on the deck of a boat, paralyzed, unable to steer, floating deeper and deeper down a dark and unfamiliar river.

8

THE TRANSITION FROM LIGHT TO DARKNESS

Time seems slower underwater. Light bends and sounds are muffled. After a while, the days just mix together. Booze, blotters, blunts, blow—*and that's just the B's.* Above me, I hear the bass thumping, rippling on the water's surface. I want so badly to breathe, but I don't remember how—

> *To the window, to the wall*
> *To the sweat drop down my balls*
> *To all these bitches crawl*
> *To all skeet skeet motherfucker,*
> *all skeet skeet god damn*

Hundreds of college kids are crammed into our house, clutching red Solo cups and grinding on each other while chanting the vile refrain. It's the same goddamn song I hear at every college party these days. It haunts my dreams and follows me wherever I go.

I even stopped going to parties just to get away from it. Now, it's blaring from the stereo system in my own living room.

The whole thing started with my roommates inviting a few friends over; but then one person told another person, who then told another person, and before we knew it, word had spread like wildfire. The conditions were just right—right people, right place, right night. Soon we had a perfect storm of a house party on our hands, a force of nature so strong that nothing can halt its path of destruction.

At some point in the night, I hear girls shrieking and spot a flurry of camera flashes erupting within the crowd. Pushing through the sea of bodies, I see Warren emerging from his lair, completely naked and sipping on a giant snifter of brandy. With a goofy smirk on his face, he walks around the party greeting guests as if he's some high-society party host. Everyone stares, speechless, with their mouths wide open. A frat bro shouts out, "Yo, who invited the naked dude?" They obviously don't realize he lives here.

That's when I recall that earlier in the night Warren asked me to keep an eye on him. "I always get naked when I'm on benzos," he said.

After a while, when everyone finally realizes that the naked dude is here to stay, Warren is not only accepted by the partygoers, but celebrated as the main attraction. Scanning the room, it's bizarre to see him mingling with the crowd—a bare-skinned beast, with blond-tinted buzzed hair, and sharp, hornlike eyebrows—the master of ceremonies leading the lost sheep.

Soon, there are people everywhere, not just in the house, but outside too, in the front yard, the backyard, the garage, and even spilling into the street. Around every corner, I find scenes of drunken chaos.

A pudgy-faced prepster puking all over the clean-clothes pile in the laundry room.

A couple of sloppy drunks making out on my bed.

Not to mention the mysterious puddles of liquid everywhere, most likely originating from the buckets of homemade hooch stationed in the kitchen.

That's where I find Chas berating a couple of unwitting stoners—"Do you have any idea how much it's going to cost me to restore this hardwood?"

In the corner, I spot Dixie lapping up one of the puddles, and that's when I finally decide that I've seen enough. I snatch up her little body and cradle it like a football while pushing through the crowd. The basement door is locked, but luckily I know another way inside.

As I carry Dixie outside to the backyard, she greets the guests with wide-eyed excitement while vigorously licking leftover hooch from her lips. Years ago, one of the previous owners built a doggy door into the cellar hatch. If you know where the handle is on the other side of the opening, you can easily reach inside and unlock the door.

Kneeling in the wet grass, I peek around to make sure that no one is watching. Once the hatch pops open, I toss Dixie inside, and she immediately scampers off into the darkness. Latching the door closed behind me, I crawl on my hands and knees along the cold, concrete floor, wiping thick spider webs off my face while maneuvering through stacked heaps of storage boxes and old gardening tools. When I feel hanging bedsheets brush against my face, I know that I've reached Warren's living room, and I gradually start making my way over to the work bench where a desk lamp is located.

Suddenly, out of darkness there is light—

Squinting, I walk over to the bookshelf and remove volume three of Gibbon's six-volume classic, *History of the Decline and Fall of the Roman Empire*, shaking loose a key hidden inside the book's spine. Sliding the shelf out of the way—revealing the hidden door—I open the lock with the key.

Meanwhile, Dixie waits breathlessly, wagging her little tail-nub; she already knows the routine. Once the door is open just enough, she squeezes inside and darts through the murky vestibule. Weaving through layers of crinkly, black plastic wrap draped from the ceiling (to block out light and smells), I can already hear the humming of the machines.

Inside the room, Dixie is rolling around in piles of shriveled-up marijuana leaves. Every now and then, as dead foliage falls off the plants, we have to rake them out of the grow machines. One of Dixie's favorite things to do is flail around in the discarded heaps.

When Warren and I first built this room, before stealing the manuscripts, we didn't know what to put inside of it. Then one day we figured, *Why not grow some weed?* So, we purchased three extra-large "vegetable grow machines"—one each for Warren, Spencer, and me. Constructed in the shape of elongated, octagonal prisms, with tinted, sliding glass panels, the devices are completely self-automated. Inside is a climate-controlled ecosystem, with internal fans to fluctuate airflow and temperature, fluorescent lights hooked up to timers, and a ten-gallon, self-feeding water tank piped directly into the soil.

Some days, I sit down here for hours just watching the plants, mesmerized by the crystally fibers reaching up to an artificial sun god, unaware that their entire world is a replication of another, existing within a hidden room in some conman's basement—universes within universes—and I can't help but think that our realities are one and the same.

Zipping open the suitcase, I carefully remove the books from their protective blankets and place them on the floor in front of me. When I want to be alone, I come down here and study the pages, using the glowing machines as reading lights. I figure it's not often I'll have the opportunity to peruse such priceless artifacts, some of which have traveled more than half a millennia, passing through the hands of various nobility to finally rest here with me on this dingy basement floor—like *Hortus Sanitatis,* the first encyclopedia of natural history, which dates back to the 15th century, and was made personally for King Henry VII. While leafing through the old vellum pages, I've discovered ornate woodcut illustrations, along with bizarre depictions of old-world creatures, like dragons, hydras, a pig-headed fish, and even a woman petting a miniature unicorn as if it were a golden retriever.

Although lately, little by little, I've been reading Darwin's *Origin of Species.* While the tone is considerably dry, the content is fascinating, which explains why the book ultimately laid the groundwork for the scientific theory of evolution. Currently, I'm in the section about variations. Darwin writes that these variations in species do not occur by chance but are somehow related to the conditions in which the species exists. Advantageous variations are naturally selected over less advantageous ones and imparted on successive generations. To support his argument, Darwin refers to animals with unused organs. There's one passage in particular that I always come back to, about cave creatures in Kentucky that ceased to evolve eyes after generations of disuse:

> On my view we must suppose that American
> Animals, having in most cases ordinary powers
> of vision, slowly migrated by successive gener-
> ations from the outer world into the deeper
> and deeper recesses of the Kentucky caves. . . .
> 'Animals not far remote from ordinary forms,
> prepare the transition from light to darkness.'

Suddenly the booming bass upstairs stops, and the place turns eerily silent. Moments later I hear a deep, muffled voice speaking. Though unable to decipher the words, I already know what he's saying, having heard the sermon many times before. There's only one thing that can stop a college party of this magnitude: the cops.

Before long, I hear someone upstairs banging on the door to the basement. I quickly bundle up the manuscripts and shove them back inside the suitcase.

Grabbing hold of Dixie, I cradle her tightly against my chest. She stares up at me with that ridiculous head-tilted, caught-lip face of hers, and I try my hardest not to burst out laughing.

Seated inside the triangle of glowing machines—with the floor, walls, and ceiling covered in black plastic wrap like infinite nothingness—I imagine that I'm stationed in the cockpit of an interstellar space-craft hurtling through the cosmos. *I can be anywhere,* I tell myself, while blocking out the noise from up above—the violent banging, the persistent pulling on the door handle—until it fades away. Eventually, I'll drift so far that none of this will matter, and all there will be is all there ever was—endless time and space.

———

One day, Warren asks me to drive him somewhere. When I ask *where to,* he just says that we're going on a "meat run." Presuming it's some new food-dubbed slang term that I'm not familiar with, like how "dough" and "cheese" refer to money, I just say, "Yeah, sure, whatever."

A little while later he hops into my car, wearing jogging pants, a hoodie, and clutching a wad of heavy-duty trash bags. As I'm driving, he navigates—*turn here, turn there*—until finally instructing me to park the car in an alley.

"Wait here," he says. "This will only take a minute."

Stepping out of the car, Warren slips on a semi-transparent, plastic mask, and pulls the hood over his head.

"Oh fuck," I say out loud, watching in the rear-view mirror as he disappears through a nondescript door from the alleyway. I start having flashbacks of the heist—*What's happening? Am I a getaway driver? Is this what we do now?*

Then, all of a sudden, Warren bursts back out of the door with the bags fully loaded, running in the opposite direction, toward the street. Just as the door closes behind him, a man wearing a butcher's apron rushes into the alley chasing after him with a large knife.

Oh fuck. Oh fuck. Oh fuck.

Shifting the car into drive, I speed down the alley to the end of the block, hoping to cut him off.

As I pull up to the cross street, I roll down the tinted windows and frantically search for Warren. That's when I spot him high-step sprinting toward me down the sidewalk, still wearing the creepy plastic mask, with the heavy trash bags slung over his shoulder, and the knife-wielding butcher on his heels.

Reaching across the passenger seat, I pop open the door to prepare for our escape. Moments later, Warren frantically tumbles inside. As I peel a U-turn in the middle of the road, he holds onto the overhead handles, trying not to fall out of the car while the door swings violently on its hinges before slamming shut as we speed away.

"What the fuck was that, Warren?" I shout.

Gasping for air, he points to the overflowing trash bags lying on the floorboard. The only word he's able to muster is, "meat."

Back at the house, Warren empties the bags onto the living room floor, creating a large mound of individually packaged frozen steaks. "You want a sirloin or a brisket?" he laughs, while rolling around on the floor in his plunder.

From that moment on, all we eat is meat. Eventually, we degenerate into wild animals, renouncing even utensils and plates, resorting to eating the steaks straight off the grill with our bare hands while writhing in pain from the heat.

But before I know it, Warren is at it again.

One night we're at the neighborhood grocery store looking for condiments to put on our steaks. Sluggishly perusing the aisles, the two of us drift apart. Later, at the checkout register, while I'm purchasing a bottle of dry rub, I spot Warren in the frozen-food section talking with the security guard. I can't hear what they're saying, but the old man keeps pointing to Warren's torso. They go back and forth for a while, exchanging words, seemingly more and more confrontational.

I wait outside, watching the situation unfold from a foggy window. By now, the standoff has moved to the front of the store near the checkout lanes. Every time Warren tries to leave, the old man steps in his way. Soon, another store employee, a middle-aged woman wearing a wrist brace, arrives on the scene of what has now turned into a tense showdown.

Suddenly, Warren unzips his coat and pulls out a pre-packaged frozen meal. Without hesitation, the security guard drags him by his arm to an employees-only room behind the Customer Service station. At which point, the other employee rushes around the desk and starts frantically dialing a number on the phone.

With my back against the wall, I slump down to the ground in a dark corner next to an out-of-order vending machine and try to process what I've just witnessed. *Why would he just give up like that?*

Unsure of what to do, I wait—hunched over in the shadows, shivering and smoking cigarettes—but nothing happens. A few customers walk in and out of the store. That's all. Still, I refuse to leave until I know what's going on.

Finally, a police car pulls up and a burly officer walks inside the store. Moments later, as if it were just a routine pickup, he casually returns with Warren in handcuffs and positions him in the back of the squad car.

And just like that, they're gone.

———

The next day, Spencer picks Warren up from jail, and we all meet back at the house. Apparently the stolen merchandise was valued so low that he'll only have to pay a fine. As Warren retells the story, he laughs about the whole thing, brushing it off as if it were just a prank. Though I'm genuinely curious about the ordeal—or more specifically, why he surrendered—I never build up the courage to ask him about it (probably because I'm worried that I already know what his answer would be). Lately, it seems like the three of us have been wanting to get caught, and the shoplifting incident is just another example of our deteriorating state.

It's been weeks and still no word from Christie's. Although we're not entirely sure if that's a good or bad thing, the general consensus is leaning toward the latter. With every passing day, we grow more paranoid, and each of us has our own particular story to prove it.

For me, it's the day the mail lady knocks on the front door and asks for an updated list of all the occupants living in the residence.

With the door just slightly cracked, I interrogate her like a bearded, strung-out junkie, although, I guess that's sort of what I am now. "Where is this coming from?" I demand. "On whose orders? Did someone put you up to this?"

She claims it's standard US Postal Service procedure. From time to time they have to update their records to do their job effectively. "It's in everyone's best interest," she says.

"Everyone's best interest?" I repeat. *Why would she say that? Is that code? Is she trying to tell me something? Like, it would be in my best interest to cooperate with the authorities? Did they put her up to this?* I nearly ask her to blink twice if this is the case, but thankfully at the last moment I reconsider.

Everyone's best interest. . . ? I'm still repeating the phrase to myself as I close the door in her face, promising to

154

write down a list of occupants and leave it in the mailbox, even though I have no intention of doing so.

"I think she's up to no good," I later say to Warren and Spencer, through a cloudy veil of drugs, my voice muffled as if underwater.

But they're not so sure. "She could just be doing her job," they say.

In the end, there's really no way of knowing. That's how this whole paranoia thing works. Gradually, over time, it eats away at your brain like a parasite. It probably doesn't help that I dropped out of college after winter break.

When I broke the news to my family during Christmas dinner, no one seemed that surprised. Earlier in the meal, I couldn't even answer basic questions about my alleged "ski trip" in West Virginia, which is where I was supposed to have been instead of New York. Over time, it had become clear to my family that I was living some sort of double life. Now, out of the blue, I drop this bomb on them that I'm taking a semester off from college. That's how I worded it—*taking a semester off*—to soften the blow. I told them that I needed to get my head on straight.

"Maybe I'll backpack through Europe," I said, that old chestnut.

In the end, it was kind of sad how quickly everyone endorsed my decision, as if they didn't think I was capable of graduating.

"You know, college isn't for everyone," my dad said, between heaping mouthfuls of sweet potato casserole.

But I knew what he really meant by this.

Growing up, there was always a stigma about not going to college, as if there was no other option after high school. It's just what you were expected to do. I remember hearing stories about friends' older siblings "taking a semester off" like it was code for having failed at life. Although it was always followed by a cute little catch phrase of condolence: "College isn't for everyone," they would say, while pitying them behind their backs.

At least now I have all the time in the world to sit around the house and concoct paranoid plots, of which it would seem there is no shortage.

One day, Warren comes rushing into the house, completely out of breath, saying that he spotted a suspicious character, dressed in a trench coat and sunglasses, lurking around the house. Apparently, he chased him down the street, where the mysterious man jumped into the back of an unmarked van and sped off.

As Warren excitedly reenacts the story, Spencer and I shoot each other smirks of skepticism. Maybe it's due to the fact that the man was dressed exactly like a stereotypical detective, or because the scene unfolded like a hardboiled crime-fiction plot in an old pulp magazine. Either way, over the years we've learned to take Warren's stories with a grain of salt.

"I promise," he says. "It really happened!"

To make matters worse, Spencer has a story of his own, which may even take the cake. He maintains that the authorities have planted undercover agents in Transy classrooms posing as students to investigate the robbery. He doesn't have any evidence to back up this theory, other than that a couple new students were suddenly enrolled in courses after the semester had already begun. It's a small school, and these kinds of things rarely go unnoticed. Plus, he says students have been asking around to see if anyone knows anything about the robbery. Not to mention, the university sent out a school-wide email appealing for information about the crime.

If true, the news is surely unsettling. Though with Spencer, you never can tell. For as long as I've known him, he's always been a paranoid creature, often hatching elaborate plots out of thin air. Although, he categorically denies these claims, alleging to possess, in his words, "a healthy amount of paranoia."

"A healthy amount of paranoia?" I ask. "Like, when you thought we were going to kill you on the Appalachian Trail?"

He stares at me, speechless.

"Warren showed me your journal."

"Why were you reading my journal?" Spencer demands, turning to Warren.

"Well, uh," Warren searches for an answer while staring me down. "You kind of left it sitting out one day, so I took a peek."

"Oh, you *took a peek*, did you?" Spencer mocks him, sarcastically. "Well, if it was just a peek, then I guess that makes it all right!"

"Did you really think that we were going to kill you?" I ask, bringing the conversation back to the matter at hand.

Spencer looks down at the ground, ashamed. "I may have thought that it was a possibility," he says.

"Why would you think that?" I ask.

"Well," Spencer says, searching for the right words. "I thought that maybe you guys didn't think I had what it took to go through with the heist, and seeing how I was the only other person who knew about it, and you kept luring me up steep cliffs, I thought that maybe you were going to push me off."

"Push you off?" Warren and I erupt at once.

"You thought we were going to push you off a mountain?" I repeat.

"We were backpacking," Warren adds. "That's the whole point, to go up mountains!"

"I know," Spencer says, shaking his head in shame. "Maybe the drugs got to me."

"Like right now?" I ask. "With this whole thing about undercover agents in your school?"

Still, Spencer maintains that it's real.

Most nights, out of paranoia, he locks himself away in his dorm room and paints, while Warren and I wander from bar to bar, popping painkillers and downing large quantities of bourbon. Occasionally, we run into old high school friends. Judging by the way they look at us, it's clear that we've crossed a line that there's no coming back from.

On one such night, Warren is surfing on the roof of my car as I drive up and down Main Street with the windows rolled down in thirty-degree weather, smoking cigarettes and listening to Malian folk music. I honk my horn and wave at the crowds of people standing outside of the bars. Some of them cheer as we drive by, but most look visibly concerned.

While stopped at a red light, a man suddenly appears outside of my window in the middle of the street.

"Take the key out of the ignition," he says.

"Excuse me?" I respond, turning down the music and looking around to see where he came from.

"I'm a police officer," he says. "Now take the key out of the ignition."

"Where's your uniform?" I ask, looking him up and down. He's dressed in normal street clothes, jeans and a jacket.

Anticipating trouble, Warren climbs down from the roof, slips through the window, and settles into the passenger seat. He startles me at first, I'd forgotten he was even up there.

"I'm off duty," the man says. "But I've already called it in. The police are on their way."

I stare at him, perplexed, as if I were trying to solve a difficult math problem. I can't figure out if he's telling the truth or just bullshitting. However, if he really did call it in, then I probably don't have much time left. The car is still running. All I would have to do is shift into drive and peel out.

Sensing my thought process, the man grabs onto my door while his other hand reaches for something out of view at his waist, presumably a pistol.

"I'm not going to tell you again," he says. "Take the key out of the ignition."

Suddenly, two police cars round the corner with their sirens blaring and screech to a halt in the middle of the street—*seems like overkill, if you ask me.*

The man walks over and apprises the officers of the situation, periodically pointing in our direction as he recounts the story, before vanishing back into the night just as quietly as he appeared.

Three officers approach from behind, shining bright lights into the windows and ordering us to show our hands while exiting the vehicle.

Once we're outside, they tell Warren to sit down on the curb. Now that I can see them up close, I'm shocked by how massive they are, like contenders on the '90s TV show *American Gladiators* ready to battle in the arena. At first, I didn't even realize that one of them was a woman, on account of her herculean frame. For identification purposes, I'll call her "Blaze," and the two male officers "Turbo" and "Cyclone."

They make me perform a series of ridiculous tests in the middle of the street, like walking heel-to-toe in a straight line, standing on one foot while touching my nose, and repeating the alphabet backward—all things that I can barely even do when I'm sober. Still, somehow I pass all of their tests, which seems to make them angry because I'm clearly drunk. So, they make me repeat the tests over and over until finally they just say that I've failed. When I ask for specifics, they refuse to give me an answer, only that I've "exhibited signs of intoxication."

After digging around in the squad car for a while, Turbo eventually returns with a breathalyzer. He fumbles with the parts before getting it assembled. Holding out the device, his only instruction is to "blow until it beeps."

Easy enough, I think.

After taking a deep breath, I blow in the general direction of the breathalyzer with my mouth about three or four inches away, assuming the gadget can detect the alcohol on my breath. (You may be surprised to learn that this is actually my first time taking a breathalyzer test; so naturally I have no idea what I'm doing.) I keep blowing, but I don't hear a beep. Meanwhile Turbo's face turns blood-red with rage.

"Put your lips on the *fucking nozzle!*" he snaps, causing me to flinch (though I try to cut him some slack, presuming it's just the steroids talking).

Now that I know what I'm doing, I put my lips on the nozzle, as instructed, and blow—but again nothing happens. Turbo angrily tells me to blow harder, even though I'm exhaling as much as physically possible. At this point, I am about to run out of breath, but I'm terrified to think of what will happen if I stop blowing. Growing dizzy, I push the remaining air out of my lungs, and at the last possible moment the device finally beeps.

Oh, thank God!

As I'm catching my breath, I see a startled look come over Turbo's face. He slowly backs away and shows the other officers the indicator screen on the breathalyzer, which I'm unable to see because it's facing away from me. While whispering to each other, the three of them form a football-like huddle, keeping their eyes on me the entire time. Based on their reactions, I'm now dying to know what my blood-alcohol level is—*maybe I broke some kind of record.*

When they leave the huddle, it's clear that their demeanor has shifted, and they've formulated some sort of game plan. They approach cautiously, talking in hushed tones, as if I'm a rabid animal they're trying to capture.

"I'm going to need you to turn around slowly and put your hands behind your back," Blaze says, enunciating each syllable slowly, as if English were not my first language.

So, that's exactly what I do, careful to keep my hands visible the entire time. As Blaze grabs my arm, I make one minor request. I've been handcuffed before, so I'm familiar with the "wrist lock" technique in which a police officer bends an arrestee's wrist to such a degree that it induces extreme pain. The tactic is supposed to be used only for subduing unruly perpetrators, but more and more it's applied in everyday arrests. Recently, I got into a scuffle at a kegger when I ran into some fraternity zombies who wanted to fight me on account of the whole "frat hit" thing. Long story short, I was drunk and throwing wild haymakers, and now I can barely bend my wrist. I tell Blaze that I think my wrist is broken and politely ask her to be careful when securing the handcuffs. However, the moment I say this, a menacing smirk spreads across her face.

"Yeah, no problem," she says, while simultaneously bending my bruised and swollen wrist to a ninety-degree angle.

A breathtaking, unimaginable pain shoots up my forearm and into my body. Without thinking, purely out of reflex, I yank my arm away from her and spin around. However, before I pulled away, Blaze was able to cinch a few notches of the handcuff, which now dangles forebodingly from my wrist.

Suddenly we're all moving in slow motion, our brains playing catch-up and trying to figure out how to proceed. Their eyes are fixed on the dangling hand-cuff as they frantically reach for objects on their belts. There's no time for words, only actions.

With my arms in the air, I make a wincing face that says, *Whoa, let's just hold on a second!* I want to shout out the words, but I'm unable to speak.

Blaze is the first to react (probably because she already knew what was going to happen when she bent my wrist). With shaky hands, she pulls an object from her belt and points it in my direction.

I brace for whatever is headed my way.

All of a sudden, a fine mist engulfs the air, but surprisingly I'm left untouched. Apparently Blaze, having nervously fumbled around with the pepper spray, managed to point the spigot in the wrong direction, shooting Turbo directly in the face, while Cyclone suffered the residual aftermath.

The two hulking beasts double over, clutching their faces and writhing in pain.

For a moment, Blaze stares quizzically at the mace canister, then corrects her hold and proceeds to hose me down.

Choking on the fumes, I hold up my hands to protect my face. The red fluid is everywhere—in my mouth, my nostrils, my eyes. The natural inclination is to turn away, but I need to see what's coming at me.

Without warning, Turbo plows me over like a griz-zly bear, hard and fast, pinning me down face-first in the middle of the street, with his knee lodged deep between my shoulder blades.

Assuming they're now going to take out their anger on me, I place my hands behind my back. The way I see it, the faster they handcuff me, the sooner this whole thing will be over with.

However, that's not the case.

Turbo cinches the cuffs so tightly around my wrists that my hands swell up like inflated balloons about to pop. Meanwhile, Blaze continues to unload the remainder of the pepper spray in my face at close range, even though I'm incapacitated, on the ground with my hands cuffed behind my back. Cyclone, apparently feeling left out, shoves his elbow and forearm into the back of my neck to keep my head in place against the concrete.

Just when I think I've suffered the extent of their assault, it gets even worse. To buy themselves more time (in case any witnesses are watching), they shake me around like a handcuffed rag doll, shouting, "Stop resisting!" In reality, I gave up long ago.

By now, more patrol cars are pulling up to the scene (apparently three body-building behemoths with deadly weapons weren't enough to control me), and the new cops want in on the action. They start taking turns on me, subbing in the late arrivals for the tired officers. Soon, I feel closed-fist punches landing on my torso from all directions.

"Get the fuck back on the curb!" one of them shouts, presumably at Warren, who must surely be freaking out right now. "Unless you want to end up like him."

No matter how much I submit, they won't stop. Suddenly it clicks in my mind: *So, this is what it feels like to be beaten!* Upon realizing this, something deep inside me snaps.

Dark urges like abysmal roots reach through me, through unending time, spewing from my mouth in a rapturous deluge of fury and violence. Using every bit of leverage possible, I scream and thrash about like a vile beast until I'm disoriented.

Moments later, I'm dizzy and hovering over the earth, parallel to the ground, with viselike hands grasping all over my body, adjusting their grips like a group of friends moving an unwieldy sofa.

They toss me head-first into the back of a squad car, where I crash into Warren, and then stuff my legs inside and close the door. Unable to use my hands, I take a moment to work myself upright and into the seat. Inexplicably, there's a distinct smell of piss all around me.

Outside my window, the cops are laughing and slapping each other on their backs as if they just won a softball game.

"Please tell me you saw all of that?" I ask Warren, still fuming with rage.

But he just stares at me, stone-faced and unmoving, as if in shock. I've never seen him like this before. I scan his body up and down, searching for injuries. That's when I notice his jeans are soaked through with urine, allowing me to finally pinpoint the mysterious smell.

"I thought they were going to kill you," Warren says, as he hangs his head and turns away from me.

—

The police let Warren go, but book me on all kinds of charges, like DUI, disorderly conduct, and resisting arrest. I spend the night in a jail cell, rubbing my pepper-sprayed eyes, which burn increasingly more as the alcohol wears off.

In the morning, I'm arraigned in court on a little video-conference monitor inside the county jail. The judge suspends my driver's license and orders me to pay hundreds of dollars in fines, plus complete countless hours of community service, adding a mandate to the ruling that only my parents can bail me out of jail (which receives an uproar of laughter from the roomful of shackled inmates).

With torn clothes, a bruised face, and red, swollen eyes, I argue that I've just turned eighteen years old, and therefore I'm considered an adult in the eyes of the law. But the judge has already deemed me an out-of-control teen who needs his mommy and daddy to *whip some sense into him* (as they say in the South), and isn't having any of it.

When they finally release me from jail, late in the evening, my mother is outside waiting for me. I didn't want her to see me like this, but there was no other alternative.

The drive home is uncomfortable, to say the least. My mom is clearly disappointed in me. How could she not be? She pleads with me to talk to her about what's going on in my life.

There are so many things I want to tell her, but I don't know how.

I want to tell her that I've been misled my entire life, and now I have no idea who I am.

I want to tell her that I feel an irrepressible obligation to destroy myself.

I want to tell her that I've done unspeakable things, that this arrest isn't even the worst of it, not even close.

I want to tell her that I'll be leaving this place soon, and that we may never see each other again.

Most importantly, I want to tell her that none of this is her fault.

But I don't say any of these things.

Instead, I just feed her the usual lines.

I fucked up.

I made a mistake.

I'm going to fix it.

When she drops me off back at my house, it's already nighttime again. The place is completely empty, and all the lights are turned off. Staggering through the pitch-black living room, I bump into every object imaginable—couches, tables, bookshelves—while trying to find a light switch. That's when I hear a distant whining sound coming from somewhere underneath me.

Following the strange noise, I feel my way along the wall until I reach the basement door. Creeping down the dark staircase, I grip the railing for support, guided only by a faint flicker of light cast from down below.

When I reach the basement floor, I see Warren sitting in a chair, playing his violin, illuminated by candlelight. He screeches along sadly—performing Tchaikovsky, *I think*—stopping occasionally to sip on bourbon and tune the strings, then tightly wedges the instrument between his jaw and collar bone, before starting back up again.

"We must free ourselves of these inherent bonds," he mutters over the wailing notes, dragging the bow heavily up and down the strings. Although he says the words aloud, it doesn't seem like he's speaking to me.

A framed picture of Warren's longtime girlfriend is propped up on the coffee table, facing him, as if he were playing the song to her. That's when I start putting the pieces together.

Recently the three of us—Warren, Spencer, and myself—came to the conclusion that in order to carry on with this particular way of life, we would have to sever all ties with family and friends, especially romantic relationships. In our view, we've become slaves to evolutionary designs inherently tailored to serve specific purposes of which we no longer need. These bonds only weaken our resolve and keep us from doing what needs to be done. The way we see it, if we can conquer our animal urges, then sooner or later we'll become masters of ourselves, capable of doing anything we set our minds to.

In the end, everyone agreed to the arrangement: we would simply turn off our emotions like a light switch. Warren had been grappling with having to break up with his girlfriend, but it appears he finally resolved that issue.

"We can't take them with us where we are going," he says, staring at an indeterminate corner of the basement, as if speaking directly to the darkness.

9
SUMME POTENS & CALLIDUS

The days don't begin and end like they used to, in neat organized segments, one discernible from the other. Now it's more like never-ending static on a television screen—cosmic background radiation left over from the big bang, infinitely sizzling my brain until the end of time.

Most nights I can't sleep, so my solution is to do more drugs, which plunges me deeper into the murky waters of an unnavigable dreamworld. In this place, my limbs don't work the way they're supposed to. I'm always off-balance, always reaching for something to hold onto.

At all hours, I find myself standing alone in my bedroom with the lights turned off, peeking through the blinds, spying on the outside world. Through a cloudy lens, I see and hear things that may or may not be there—shadowy figures moving in the darkness, rustling in the bushes outside my window.

I walk outside into the cold night. The screen door creaks and snaps shut behind me, echoing down the quiet, deserted street.

"I know you're out there!" I shout, laughing and pointing at black shapes, always waiting for some hidden agent to appear out of nowhere.

But nothing ever happens.

These days I go to bed fully dressed in a hoodie and sweatpants, with my running shoes tied on my feet. This way, if anyone comes for me in the middle of the night, I'll be ready to run.

I've already got the escape route planned out:

From my bedroom window, I'll make a short jump down to the grass and dart through the yard. In the back, I've cut a hole in the fence, which leads to the UK Track & Field Complex. At night, all the lights are turned off, so I can just slip into the darkness, running along the perimeter until I reach the bleachers—hopping, ducking, weaving in and out of the metal beams. After that, it's just an easy jump over the main gate, on the opposite side of the complex, where I'll disappear into a labyrinth of campus buildings.

They won't be able to keep up with me. I know the athletics complex like the back of my hand. Oddly enough, we used to practice soccer there as kids, back when Warren's dad was our coach. If I close my eyes, I can still picture the three of us—Warren, Spencer, and me—running through fields of freshly mowed grass, living moment to moment in naive bliss. I never imagined that one day I'd be on the opposite side of the fence, cutting a hole to get inside, so that I might run through those same fields, under the cover of darkness, for a different reason entirely.

During the day, I walk around campus trying to spot if I'm being followed. I stop in front of windows and stare at reflections, scanning the backdrop for suspicious-looking characters. Like that guy over there sitting alone on the bench. *What's he doing there? Does he look familiar? Or does he just have one of those faces?*

I slip into a lecture hall to see if the man follows me. Students are still filing through the doors and taking their seats. It's a large class—some sort of philosophy course—so I shouldn't stand out too much (for all intents and purposes, I still look like a normal college kid). I watch the door closely and wait until the last moment. Once the instructor starts speaking, I duck out of the classroom and scurry down a marble-floored corridor, peering back to see if anyone is following me, but no one is there.

I do this day after day, and eventually I even start sitting in on some of the classes, just for entertainment, even though I'm not enrolled in the university anymore. At first it was just a tactic to see if I was being tailed, but then I found the course material rather interesting, so I ended up staying.

In between classes, I wander around campus with no purpose or destination, drugged-up, paranoid, frantically peeking over my shoulder, as the days blend together and philosophy coursework devours my mind—

How do I know that my entire universe is not an illusion created by an omnipotent demon only to deceive me?

The only way to know something is to eliminate the possibility of it being false.

But what if my reasoning is also flawed, and therefore my thoughts untrue?

After a while, I decide that I can't take it anymore. I can't stay in this place with the same routine day after day. I've reached a tipping point, and there's no going back.

I rush to the library and sit down at the first open computer I can find. Without thinking, I buy a plane ticket to London, departing next week. While probably not the wisest destination choice, it was the most accessible European city on the list, so I immediately booked the flight, shelling out extra for round-trip airfare (to avoid suspicion), even though I have no intention of coming back.

When I first tell Warren and Spencer about what I've done, they're taken completely by surprise, but eventually they come around to the idea. Seeing how I'm the only one not enrolled in school, it seems like the perfect opportunity. Plus, I've already mentioned to family and friends that I'm planning on backpacking through Europe during my semester off, which provides a cover story.

In reality, I'll bring the manuscripts to London, while Warren arranges a meeting for me with the Amsterdam dealer. If, for some reason, I'm unable to make contact, I'll start searching for new buyers on my own. After all, how hard could it be? Warren was able to do it stateside with just an email address. At any rate, this step—getting the books to Europe—was going to have to be done at some point anyway. We might as well get it over with.

As the details of the plan sink in, Warren and Spencer struggle to conceal their sadness. Things are moving quickly, and we have to adapt. Warren promises to meet me in Europe at the end of the semester. Spencer, on the other hand, makes no such promise. The truth is, there's no need to mention what's really on everyone's mind. They already know I'm not coming back. It's clear that we've reached the end.

10

DIXIE'S DEAD

I find myself standing alone in the darkness—

The sound of an explosion echoes in my head.

Outside my room, I hear an army of pounding footsteps pouring into the house.

For some reason, I'm already dressed, with my shoes tied tightly on my feet.

I don't know how I got here. I don't remember anything before this, just remnants of a fading dream, floating like an asymptote in black ether, forever approaching a lucent plane where curved horizons meet.

Suddenly it hits me—*this is really happening.*

Peeking through the blinds into the living room, I see crisscrossing light beams and SWAT agents in tactical gear weaving through flash-grenade smoke with assault rifles drawn. They break down the door leading upstairs to Chas's room, and instantly a voice yells out, *"Drop the gun!"*

I brace for a barrage of bullets that somehow never comes.

Underneath my feet, I hear them busting through the cellar door, screaming, *"Federal search warrant!"*

as they descend upon the basement and Warren's bedroom.

That's when I realize that nobody knows I'm back here, otherwise they would've come for me already. My solarium-turned-bedroom is an extension of the house. From the inside, it just looks like a back door.

Dixie's dead, I tell myself. *You knew this day would come.*

I look around the room one last time, wondering if I should take anything with me. *Laptop? Clothes? Money?* Then I remember that I don't need those things anymore—*not where I'm going*—that life is over.

I've made up my mind: no more running.

Inhaling deeply, I unlock and open the door—not thinking about what happened before this, or what will happen after—focused only on the whirlwind of steadfast light intently closing in on me.

ABOUT THE AUTHOR

Eric Borsuk is the author of *American Animals*, the memoir featured in the acclaimed motion picture of the same name. His work has appeared in such publications as *VICE Magazine* and *The Marshall Project*. He currently lives in New York City.